A Generous Openness

Praying
the Spiritual Exercises
of St. Ignatius

Charlotte C. Prather

ST. BEDE'S PUBLICATIONS
Petersham, Massachusetts

Published by: St. Bede's Publications
P.O. Box 545
Petersham, Massachusetts 01366-0545
5   4   3   2   1

LIBRARY OF CONGRESS CATALOGING-IN-PUBLICATION DATA

Prather, Charlotte Carroll, 1947-
   A generous openness : praying The spiritual exercises of St.
Ignatius / Charlotte C. Prather.
      p. cm.
   Includes bibliographical references.
   ISBN 0-932506-85-2
   1. Spiritual life—Catholic authors. 2. Prayer—Catholic
Church. 3. Ignatius, of Loyola, Saint, 1491-1556. Exercitia
spiritualia. 4. Spiritual exercises. 5. Prather, Charlotte
Carroll, 1947-   . I. Title.
BX2350.2.P6472   1991
248.3--dc20   90-47875
                                                             CIP

CONTENTS

For my father,
Charles C. Carroll
(1916-1986)

Acknowledgments

I wish to thank the faculty at the Weston School of Theology whose classes were informed by Ignatian spirituality, and most especially Fr. Joseph E. McCormick, S.J., who shared with me his friendship with St. Ignatius and guided me through the *Spiritual Exercises*. I appreciate particularly the encouragement, patience, and wisdom of my pastor and friend, Fr. Reginald A. Redlon, O.F.M., who read every word of the manuscript as it was being written. Finally, my deep gratitude goes to all those who supported and bore with me during the writing of this book—my colleagues at St. Anne's Parish in Fair Lawn, New Jersey, all the friends who kept prodding me to finish this work, and my family who loved me through it all: my husband, Michael, and our sons, John and Matthew. May God reward them in ways that I cannot even imagine.

Introduction

This book is the result of an improbable friendship: mine with St. Ignatius Loyola. Although all I knew about the life of Ignatius, when I first entered into the extraordinary spiritual journey called a "Nineteenth Annotation Retreat," was that he had been a soldier and founded the Society of Jesus, I soon came to love him as he emerges in the pages of his greatest work, the *Spiritual Exercises*.

It was never the intention of Ignatius to write a book which would simply be read and studied, nor did he envision anyone praying through the Exercises in a solitary and undirected way. They are, in fact, a set of instructions for a director who will present the Exercises to a retreatant during the course of a thirty-day retreat. Ignatius includes a list of "annotations," guidelines for the proper conduct of the retreat. It was the nineteenth annotation which attracted my attention, in that it presented the possibility of undertaking the Exercises over an extended period of time while one carried on one's normal activities and responsibilities. For most people, the freedom to make a thirty-day retreat is a luxury not to be taken for granted. When I began the nineteenth annotation, I was married, studying theology, doing pastoral field education, translating, and raising two little boys.

Nothing had prepared me for the experience I was about to have, and I did not read the *Spiritual Exercises* in advance to find out what I might expect. In my naive enthusiasm, I had thought this would be a nice "project" for Lent. Sight unseen (in a true sense), I asked someone whose experience and wisdom I trusted to direct me in a nineteenth annotation retreat. Lent began and ended, but I was engaged in a "project" which would take considerably longer and radically change my way of seeing things. The *Spiritual Exercises* usually do take quite a long time in this form, but in a sense I never finished them (although technically I did reach the end). They have become a part of me, their various "weeks" and meditations being a kind of horizon against which I can see and reflect upon the course of my life, and to which I return again and again.

The chapters which follow are a description of the *Spiritual Exercises* of St. Ignatius as I experienced them. I shall attempt to present the internal dynamic process which takes place in the person doing the Exercises, to give a view of this process *from within*. It is not my intention to write either a literary or a theological analysis of Ignatius' work. There already exists a formidable body of scholarly writing on the *Spiritual Exercises*. I wish simply to describe the experience of entering into Ignatius' meditations and to tell the stories of God's goodness which I encountered in the course of them.

The stories which are the heart of this book are, for the most part, my own. A few have been graciously told me by others. Some are composites. Not all were experienced in the context of the Exercises, but later appeared to be particularly illuminating of one or the other Exercise. I tell of my own experience of grace because it is the only one I truly know *from within*. I hope, however, that what is here related has much more to say about God's ways of meeting and loving a human person, than about me in particular. Similarly, it is my belief that the *Spiritual Exercises*, which form the framework of this book, are of interest today, not because they represent an esoteric system of prayer and asceticism, but because they bring one into a vital encounter with the Gospel of Jesus Christ, into a genuine dialogue with the living God. Such a dialogue is always life-giving and profoundly transforming.

A Church History professor of mine once pointed out that St. Anselm did not write the *Proslogion*, containing his famous ontological proof for the existence of God, in order to *prove* God (which he would have considered unnecessary), but to *praise* God. Faith was a given for him. He sought to enlighten the mind regarding that faith, and to do so in a very beautiful way—to present to the Creator a writing as beautifully crafted as a stained glass window or a lovely piece of music. In choosing to write a book about the *Spiritual Exercises* of St. Ignatius, I have a purpose similar to St. Anselm's—that is, I wish not to explain or to analyze Ignatius' great work, but to rejoice in it, as in a gift from a friend. I offer this writing in deepest gratitude and with the hope that it may find a place with all the statues and music and colored windows which exist only to give pleasure and praise to God.

A GENEROUS OPENNESS

Chapter One
The "Principle and Foundation"

At the threshold of the *Spiritual Exercises*, Ignatius has placed a short preface which gives the premise upon which all that follows shall rest, and which gives meaning and direction to the entire course of the Exercises. His preface (with some small alterations which I have made for the sake of a verbal expression of humankind which is more inclusive of women and also more corporate) reads as follows:

> Men and women are created to praise, reverence, and serve God our Lord, and to receive the grace of salvation.
> And the other things on the face of the earth are created for the human family, that they may help it in prosecuting the end for which it is created. From this it follows that men and women are to use them as much as they help towards this end, and ought to rid themselves of them so far as they hinder them as to it.
> For this it is necessary to make ourselves indifferent to all created things in all that is allowed to the choice of our free will and is not prohibited to it; so that, on our part, we want not health rather than sickness, riches rather than poverty, honor rather than dishonor, long rather than short life, and so in all the rest; desiring and choosing only what is most conducive for us to the end for which we are created. [23][1]

The few sentences which comprise this "Principle and Foundation" are so simple and, to a reflective Christian, so self-evident that one might be tempted to read over them quickly in the hope of soon arriving at something more interesting. That would be a serious mistake, however, for here, in this short catechetical passage, lies the heart of the matter: the human person's relationship to God and to the rest of creation ("the other things"). We have a tendency to forget that we too are part of creation. But Ignatius reminds us of our creaturely status and our purpose: ". . . to praise, reverence, and serve God our Lord." This goal is not to be achieved in solitary isolation but in the midst of and in interaction with the created reality around us, all of which, says Ignatius, has been given in order that we might attain to our primary end.

The grace which one may glimpse hidden behind these preliminary sentences is the freedom to be able to relate to other creatures in a way that will lead us to the praise and service of the Lord. Essentially, we need to be able to see God in all of creation, and yet at the same time be able to go beyond our relationship to it and not possessively substitute it for the God of whom we initially heard it speak. That all of creation and especially the beauty of the earth are able to be transparent to transcendent Beauty, and that there is in the human being the capacity to look through this glass, to see and to worship in its reflection the God whom no one has seen, is amply attested to in the psalms. To hear the words of adoration and wonder of the psalmist, to allow these words to be spoken at the deepest level of the heart, is a good way to enter upon the *Spiritual Exercises.*

> The heavens declare the glory of God,
>   and the firmament proclaims his handiwork.
> Day pours out the word to day,
>   and night to night imparts knowledge;
> Not a word nor a discourse
>   whose voice is not heard;
> Through all the earth their voice resounds,
>   and to the ends of the world, their message.
>   (Ps. 19:2-5)

The poetry of the psalms, actually liturgical songs, has the capacity to move and reorient the one who prays them because they address not only the intellect but (in the most unsentimental sense possible) the heart. The beauty and power of words and images awaken in us an aesthetic and an affective response which engages the will and the feelings. Because of this, we pray in ways which are not merely discursive. We come to a deeper and more realistic knowledge of who we are—of who we are in relationship to God. We begin, in fact, to know God. But this knowing is not the rational knowledge of the intellect, but the knowledge of love and of faith which is the gift of the Holy Spirit.

The entry into the spirit of the "Principle and Foundation" is not limited to the access given in the passion and beauty of the psalms, however. For Ignatius, God was to be seen in everything. Anything which can open our eyes to that kind of seeing is used in order to help us attain our end. One might just as profitably listen to music, play with children, rake leaves, or watch airplanes take off, providing only that these things do not hold us in an obsessive attachment but rather open us to the experience of gratitude and praise which is truly the foundation upon which these Exercises are built. For me, that has most often been the case with the loveliness of the earth, of mountains, woods, night skies, daytime skies, and water in all its amazing forms.

One year, in the late summer, I spent some time with my family in the Rocky Mountains of Colorado. The children and I would take gentle hikes in the mountains for a couple of hours each morning. One afternoon, however, feeling extremely restless and unable to settle down to anything, I decided to go walking by myself. The family had undergone a number of major changes (a move to a new state, new jobs, new schools) and the summer had been a tiring and disorganized one. I was not at all sure about the directions my life would be taking in the future, and certainly had no simple and unambiguous sense of the paths along which God might be leading me. In a word, I was confused. Not only did I have no clear answer to all my questions; I did not even know what all the questions were. I felt burdened by the weight of all the subject matter in my life and yearned for some clarity and meaning to emerge from the experiential overload of the previous few months.

Frustrated by my inability to organize mentally all the various strands of my own and my family's life history, I set out to walk up a dirt road used for maintenance vehicles during the ski season. It was not strenuous hiking except for the fact of high altitude and I had determined to go as far as I reasonably could in one afternoon. At first I walked along quite vigorously, noticing the beauty all around but not being really touched by it. I was impatient and conscious of wishing I were able to think and pray more "coherently" about my very large "agenda." I was undoubtedly expecting to come back with some clear answers, while still feeling irritated at not being able to formulate the questions properly.

As I marched along purposefully, I thought with a certain amount of amusement of the long history of those who have gone up various mountains in their search for God. But the one figure who presented himself most vividly to my mind was St. Francis of Assisi on Mt. Alvernia. I remembered that the God Francis had met on that mountain was the crucified Christ. I found myself very moved by the sudden recollection of St. Francis on the mountain. Beyond that, I neither knew, thought, nor prayed anything more specific. But that one very brief insight produced a remarkable change in me. I felt peaceful and consoled. Not one of my questions had been answered; I still was not very sure of the questions themselves. What was amazing was that they no longer seemed at all significant. And there were other changes. My walking became more leisurely and pleasurable. I felt like a part of the landscape, related to earth and grass, rather than like an alien taking it by storm. My attention was caught and held by what I had merely noticed before. Even the grasshoppers became much more interesting to me. (In fact, I had not even noticed their presence up until this moment.)

I continued my climb along the maintenance road which, at one point, grew very steep. Being used only to sea-level, I considered this to be a serious challenge. By the time the slope had become more gradual again, I was quite parched and sunbaked. A few hundred yards later, I was astonished to come upon a waterfall—just a small one but very beautiful in the sun. It is generally not safe to drink from mountain streams or I would surely have done so. As it was, I was drawn to the water which was crystal clear and icy from the melting snows high up on the peaks. I balanced on a rock to scoop up handfuls of it and pour it over my head. For the first time I understood "in my flesh" why water is so often used as an image for God in the Bible. These were, in a real and physical sense, living waters and I doused myself until my hair, clothes, and even shoes were wet. Dripping, squishy, and full of thanksgiving, I went on my way, grateful also for the hot Colorado sun which was now pleasantly warm.

Still damp from my rebirth, I left the road and went back down to the village through grassy meadows full of daisies and many other wildflowers whose names I did not know. Once I realized that I was really away from any other human beings (a rare event for an easterner and city-dweller), I started singing as I clumped down the gentle hills and found my way home by means of ski trail signs. Later I asked myself what had happened. I had no answers. I still was not sure of the questions, although I knew that I would have to deal with them in the months ahead. But I returned home praising God. And that is what I was created to do.

Already in the "Principle and Foundation," Ignatius presents key concepts which will function throughout the course of the Exercises and beyond: freedom and choice. The fundamental choice to be made, "to praise, reverence, and serve God our Lord," can only take place in a state of freedom. It is important that this fundamental choice does not represent some esoteric knowledge or special ascetical practice peculiar to his "system." It is wholly biblical and basic to both the Hebrew and the Christian Scriptures. It is not necessary that the present reader have made the *Spiritual Exercises* or even read them. One might simply understand the "Principle and the Foundation" as a meditation on these words:

> The LORD is our God, the LORD alone! Therefore, you shall love the LORD, your God, with all your heart, and with all your soul, and with all your strength. Take to heart these words which I enjoin on you today. Drill them into your children. Speak of them at home and abroad, whether you are busy or at rest. Bind them at your wrist as a sign and let them be as a pendant on your forehead. Write them on the doorposts of your houses and on your gates.
>
> (Deut. 6:4-9)

The relationship to created things is critical to the relationship to God. The Old Testament authors are primarily concerned with the danger idolatry poses to the exclusive worship of God. For Ignatius, idolatry occurs through disordered relationships to created things, relationships which strangle freedom and leave us unable to live the life for which we were created. An act of the will, for instance, will not automatically enable a person to praise, reverence, and serve the Lord. Idolatry with regard to "the other things" has chained the human will. One may discover (in the attempt to praise, reverence, and serve the Lord) that one is preoccupied, distracted, bored, angry, anxiety-ridden, and guilty. In fact, all of these feelings may be found within most of us, at times simultaneously. If, by some miracle, it becomes possible to look with serenity upon the past and the future (an unlikely "if," to be sure), then there are bound to rise up sufficient idols from our present daily contexts, idols which stand between us and the God who desires to draw us closer. The idols assert themselves insistently.

It is thus that we find ourselves unfree, bound to the rest of creation in ways that are contradictory, confusing, and often sinful. Moreover, we may even be enslaved to parts of our own personality and life history: to needs and desires, unresolved feelings and dependencies, likes and dislikes. These too are some of "the other things" which are (most often unconsciously) worshipped. This is the situation, described so painfully by St.Paul, of those who do not yet live in the freedom of the Holy Spirit, but are still at the mercy of the warring forces within them:

> What I do, I do not understand. For I do not do what I want, but I do what I hate. . . . For I do not do the good I want, but I do the evil I do not want. . . . For I take delight in the law of God, in my inner self, but I see in my members another principle at war with the law of my mind, taking me captive to the law of sin that dwells in my members (Rom. 7:15-23).

That which is not God, both within us and external to us, is often the object of desire. Out of neediness and attachment, we fall into idolatry. The beauty of the world which was meant to be a transparent glass through which men and women might glimpse their Creator (however darkly) has become an opaque screen.

To counteract this condition of bondage, Ignatius develops the concept of indifference, an idea which can be somewhat confusing at first. It is important not to misunderstand Ignatian indifference as apathy or stoicism—and least of all as dispassionate coldness. The word only makes sense in the context of a great desire and a passionate love for God, to which all other desires and loves are subordinated. The use of any created thing and, more importantly, the choice of any act is to be governed solely by the criterion of "the end for which we are created."

The ordering principle of indifference should by no means be construed as a prohibition against loving creatures. In his instructions for making a good election (a choice among good alternatives), Ignatius uses the image of a balance scale. One must hold oneself equally balanced between the two things and then allow oneself to be led by grace and reason towards that choice which is *more* for the service and praise of God. Having made a choice, one is then to *embrace* it, love God in it, and love it because of the love of God (which is in no sense an "indifferent" sort of love).

Ignatius is very straightforward and honest in his presentation of the necessity for indifference, although he can hardly have expected one who was beginning the Exercises for the first time to have already attained it. In a sense, one enters upon this path with the goal, the praise and service of God, already in view, precisely because the route one will travel is a matter of choice. At each point, a new dimension of freedom (indifference) is needed in order to be able to choose the end (love) which has been seen and embraced from the beginning (faith).

From the start of the Exercises then, there is a configuration which will remain present throughout in a variety of forms: God, the person praying (making the Exercises), and the rest of created reality. It is now possible to become increasingly aware of those "other things" which obscure the vision of God. The "idols" are both internal and external. We cling to possessions, power, prestige, excitement, glamour, and other persons. We also tend to live in the service of inner disorders: fear, anxiety, guilt, dependencies of all kinds, anger, lust, and the need to control (ourselves, our environment, and other people). Our likes and dislikes, desires and aversions, can exercise demonic power over us.

Let us return now to the situation of my hike in Colorado. At the start of the walk, I was by no means indifferent. In fact, I could only see "the other things": my anxiety, confusion, and all the many questions. The face of God was wholly obscured by them. These internal facts were my personal idols of the moment. At the same time there were also "the other things" external to me, which in fact functioned for me in a proper creative relationship. Eventually the silence, the solitude, the enormity of the mountains, and the tiny fragility of some of their living inhabitants, as well as the healing beauty and refreshment of the water, broke through the wall of turmoil in my mind and spoke directly to my heart of their and my Creator. I loved them: the walking, the beautiful place, the quiet time. They had been, in fact, the agents of my freedom, nudging me towards a greater indifference. What I learned was that my bondage to questions and anxiety had kept me insulated and unable to experience my present circumstances. Freed of those questions and that anxiety (i.e., indifferent to them), I could enjoy the moment and its beauty. To be free is to live more abundantly *now*. Jesus says that is why he has come (John 10:10).

Note

[1]David L. Fleming, S.J., *The Spiritual Exercises of St. Ignatius: A Literal Translation and a Contemporary Reading*, (St.Louis: Institute of Jesuit Sources, 1978), [23]. Further references to Ignatius' literal text will be made by the use of brackets immediately following the citations.

Chapter Two
Sin and Grace: The "First Week"

"I was naked and you clothed me"

The meditations on sin which Ignatius proposes for the "first week" will probably not be an easy matter for most people. In the first Exercise one is asked to consider three sins: that of the angels, that of Adam and Eve, and finally any grave sin which results in damnation. Of these three, the first and third may appear especially elusive. The form of meditation required here is an intellectual and discursive one, for which it might be better to think in terms of conceptualization than imagination. The very abstract quality of these particular Exercises may seem daunting to those used to more specificity and concreteness in their creative imaginings. Even the sin of Adam and Eve is more easily understood as symbol than history. It is an emblem of sin and lacks the particularity (with which we can identify) of the sin of Cain or of King David, for instance.

There is, however, a substantial biblical text surrounding the sin of Adam and Eve which provides some support for meditation. Ignatius mentions, for instance, that the first parents are clothed in garments of skin and are cast out of Paradise. The original nakedness of these human beings and their subsequent need for clothing are striking details: they hide themselves in shame; God very graciously and *patiently* clothes them. The image of nakedness and clothing is very powerful. We wear clothes for reasons beyond warmth and cultural concepts of decency. Our bodies are, in fact, the physical reality of our vulnerability. After infancy, very few people willingly appear naked except before someone whom they greatly trust. The free giving and receiving of one another's nakedness (and also of mutual vulnerability) may be seen as a more certain sign of genuine love between two people than the mere fact of an active sexual relationship (which may be indicative of many other things besides love). For this reason, it is usually considered such an extreme violation of human dignity to strip prisoners of their clothing, a practice of which there are notorious examples in our century.

In a sinful condition, one must of necessity hide oneself. In a condition of very grave sin, the hiddenness amounts to absolute self-banishment: the prideful angels from the presence of God, the unrepentant sinner to the depths of hell. All of us, consciously or unconsciously, attempt to hide the fact of our sin from others, from ourselves, and ultimately from the very eyes of God. We may be willing to admit sin intellectually, but to experience it as part of who we are, at the core of our being, is another matter. To grasp it, to hold it in our hands, to bring it into the presence of another person, to expose it to the light of God in Christ requires a willingness to be naked which is quite terrifying. Thus, like Adam and Eve, we take cover under the trees of denial and repression and persuade ourselves that to hide from the face of God is less painful than to experience our shame. The lengths to which we will go in deception and self-deception are vividly depicted in the Book of Isaiah:

Your lips speak falsehood,
    and your tongue utters deceit.
No one brings suit justly,
    no one pleads truthfully;
They trust in emptiness and tell lies;
    they conceive mischief and bring forth malice.
They hatch adders' eggs,
    and weave spiders' webs:
Whoever eats their eggs will die,
    if one of them is pressed, it will hatch as a viper;
Their webs cannot serve as clothing,
    nor can they cover themselves with their works.
                                            (Is. 59:3-6)

Like witnesses before our own inner court, we falsify the evidence. We put lies between ourselves and God, and do this so easily that we do not even notice that we do it. Even in the moment of confessing our guilt, we may let some seductive form of deception fall like a veil or filter over our true self.

The defenses we use to protect ourselves from a conscious encounter with our sin may be compared to the wrappings around a victim of third degree burns. If that is so, then a grace of the first week would be to experience the removal of all those layers of gauze which not only hide our wounds from view, but also insulate them (and us) from healing, forgiveness, and love. God does not tear away our bandages by force, but is gentle and kind, and allows us to do so ourselves according to the time-table of our own readiness. Like our first parents, we have left Paradise, but we have been given the courtesy of protective clothing. It is only in our freedom that we may someday unveil ourselves before Someone whom we love and trust, but that will happen when we have experienced that Someone has loved and trusted *us* enough to allow us that freedom. Often we discover that we do not even love and trust ourselves enough to take this first step.

The War of Resistance

The self-knowledge which results from such an unveiling can be very frightening. It is also the prerequisite for any spiritual growth. There are forces in most people which fight vigorously against any change and, therefore, react to growth in self-awareness as to a lethal threat. All that we have become up until now struggles to survive and to maintain itself over against new growth. Essentially, the emergence of the new creation which is the work of the Holy Spirit in us, means death to the status quo, the old Adam and Eve who are, however, much too self-satisfied and complacent to die without a great struggle.

At times the experience of such enormous inner struggle may indeed be likened to warfare. The person whose soul is the battlefield for this encounter is intensely aware of internal conflict, turmoil, and ambiguity. Ignatius writes at the beginning of his section on the "General Examen of Conscience":

I presuppose that there are three kinds of thoughts in me: that is, one my own, which springs from my mere liberty and will; and two others, which come from without, one from the good spirit, and the other from the bad. [32]

It may seem to the person doing the Exercises that all three of these sources of thought are rampaging within. At other times, one is barely conscious of any inner response at all, or may even experience feelings of restlessness, boredom, and almost insurmountable sleepiness while doing the Exercises. Both of these types of response, the embattled as well as the disengaged, represent an experience of resistance. This is neither unexpected nor "bad" in any way, but rather a normal and alive response to the requirement of honest self-examination which underlies the first week.

The second Exercise, for instance, in calling for a stage-by-stage review of one's entire life history, should evoke some form of resistance. In fact, the absence of resistance could well be an indication that the subject matter is not being seriously engaged, that the Exercise is being only superficially performed. The *Spiritual Exercises* are a series of dynamic encounters, not a pious ritual. The initial self-confrontations in the Exercises on sin ought not normally to be peaceful ones. One may sit down comfortably in one's favorite "praying chair" only to discover that one can hardly bear to stay there. There seems to be no ability to concentrate, meditate, or even sit still. Distractions may be experienced as charging through the mind like subway commuters at rush hour.

In such a state of distraught restlessness, one will hardly be conscious of the presence of God. Ignatius recommends a change of posture. Sometimes lying prostrate or walking around will help to focus an unruly and resistant mind. This is so because we are very incarnational creatures. What we do with our bodies not only reflects but actually *is* a reality. To kneel before our Creator is a true act of worship even when our brain wants to plan a dinner menu, outline the next chapter of a book, or even fall asleep. The physicality of bodily gestures of reverence may bring the wandering mind into the moment of worship as well.

The experience of restlessness and even of disconnectedness and alienation is not an inappropriate one for these Exercises dealing with sin. We are discovering the pain of separation from love. The one thing which we may desire, enjoy, and indulge in to our heart's content is the presence of God. Karl Rahner writes of the wild extravagance of loving God:

> In loving Your holy Immensity, our ordinary life of enforced moderation and proportion becomes tolerable. In You the heart can safely follow its yearning for the limitless, can wander aimlessly without going astray. I can prodigally lavish my affections on every single aspect of Your Being, and find in each of them everything I see¹ ⁓ᵘse everything in You is the whole.¹

Like   ' ⁓ dreadful absence of God is a genuine
exₚ   ⁓ᵢₙ. for the disorientation, unrest,
aₙ   .he experience of having lost
ₜ   gives us meaning, peace, and
          ᴐd in prayer is a very precious
         .at we would rather suffer any
ᴐ.   d delight in the Lord becomes
somethₙ.ᵧ   .nore. This is grace.

Applying the Senses

As we begin to appreciate more consciously the nature of our relationship with God, so too, conversely, the emptiness and misery that is sin also begins to become more palpably real to us. In this first week, the fifth Exercise, which throughout the course of the *Spiritual Exercises* is an "application of the senses," is a meditation on hell. Ignatius instructs us to apply our vision, hearing, sense of taste, smell, and touch to the reality of hell (or during the later weeks to whatever mystery in the life of Jesus is the subject for meditation). How this is to be done is matter for the creative imagination of the person praying and, of course, the work of the Holy Spirit. That it is something which can be

really experienced in prayer is undoubtedly true. St. Teresa of
Avila records a vivid and terrifying vision of hell:

> ...while I was in prayer one day, I suddenly found that, without
> knowing how, I had seemingly been put in hell.... The entrance it
> seems to me was similar to a very long and narrow alleyway, like an
> oven, low and dark and confined; the floor seemed to me to consist
> of dirty, muddy water emitting a foul stench and swarming with
> putrid vermin. At the end of the alleyway a hole that looked like a
> small cupboard was hollowed out in the wall; there I found I was
> placed in a cramped condition. All of this was delightful to see in
> comparison with what I felt there.[2]

Perhaps for a contemporary person, a realistic scenario of
nuclear war would be equally effective (and affecting). Any
experiential knowledge of the suffering caused by sin and of the
void which it creates may be applied here. One might undertake
a reading of the testimony at the Nuremberg trials.

Sin, for the person who seeks the holiness of God, is an ugly
matter. If it is experienced as upsetting, unpleasant, and a source
of inner turbulence, then there is a prospect for real spiritual
growth to take place. It is for this reason that the repetitions and
the application of senses which Ignatius prescribes for the Exercises are so important. The initial encounter is highly informa-
tive to one who is aware of inner responses, both positive and
negative. In the repetitions, those areas which evoked such
responses can be much more profoundly "contemplated." And
in the application of senses, we come to know in our flesh that
which we have contemplated.

The various responses to the Exercises on sin in their repeating patterns may be experienced, for example, as a struggle
between conflicting feelings of desire and fear: the desire for
grace and the will of God, on the one hand, and the fear of the
consequences of grace, on the other. If nothing else, by this
point, we shall have become well aware of this ambivalence and
contradiction present in our innermost being, an awareness
which, because it approaches truth, brings us closer to authentic
humility. There may be times, however, when one feels in real
danger of annihilation because of this. The fear of unknown

changes which will undoubtedly result from this prayer can be very powerful.

What may keep me from a despairing capitulation to this overwhelming fear is the knowledge given by faith (itself a grace) that God's love and grace is greater than my confusion and ambivalence, and certainly greater than my sin. Out of this love and grace, not out of my efforts at meditation (however successful or unsuccessful they may seem to me), will come inevitably change, and not necessarily change as I have envisioned and feared it. Rather, the change will appear to me precisely *as* grace, perhaps in the form of a new openness and willingness to see and allow whatever it is that God intends to do with me in and through these Exercises. I may find myself willing to feel whatever feelings (or absence of feelings) may result from them, and even let go a bit of my desire to control the outcome, or at least to know in advance what that outcome is going to be.

Finding the Hidden One

Reflective people might argue that they are quite aware of their past sins and failings and have no need of meditative exercises to inform them about their own life histories. The problem with our self-knowledge, however, is that it is often a knowledge *only* of the mind. It does not affect our actual, tenaciously held self-image, usually a quite idealized and not very realistic self which is all our ego is able to recognize. Our real self is perhaps very neglected, hardly ever seen, and not at all loved and accepted. This poor orphan is the creature of God whom in our prayer we come to meet, begin to know intimately, and, finally, love (in its weaknesses as well as its strengths).

It should not be surprising, however, if the first encounters with this deeply closeted real self are characterized more by reluctance, denial, and rejection than by loving acceptance. How can we willingly identify with this creature whom we are not sure that even a mother could love? And yet *this* is the one whom God has first loved, not our false self-image which has, after all, no reality. How could the One who is all Truth love any but our true self? It is this sinful but real self about whom we learn during the first week. The Exercises dealing with sin allow us to become aware of our spiritual corruption and impoverishment. We begin to experience sin as conscious and willful, rather than unconscious and accidental, or even inevitable. This experience is one which can be very painful. We feel that our condition is a miserable one indeed.

It is necessary to stress the importance of the verbal and dialogic structural elements of the *Spiritual Exercises*. In fact, the rather elaborate forms of the Exercises, with their preludes, points, and colloquies, function to enable a conversation to take place between the person praying and God.[3] In a sense, the "script" of the one doing the Exercises might be seen as quite rigidly dictated. The divine end of the dialogue remains open, however, and since that is so, then in fact the entire dialogue is really and amazingly unique, for God's participation in human events, whether corporate or personal, is always experienced as new and illuminating.

It is a matter of good faith and generosity that we who do the Exercises actually follow Ignatius' guidelines. It requires a certain openness, for instance, to request in the very first Exercise the grace that one might feel "shame and confusion" about one's sins. After all, most of us spend a great deal of time avoiding whole categories of negative, bad, unacceptable, and "unwanted" feelings. Shame certainly falls into this group, representing as it does an almost unbearable loss of self-esteem. At the outset, then, an opening onto previously closed regions of our own inner terrain is made available. The feeling of shame and confusion is not created in us by the *Spiritual Exercises*. Rather, we come to notice and to *feel* what was hidden and repressed within us all along. The activation of such feelings allows for the beginning of a process of awareness, growth, and conversion.

There is another reason for this very first prayer for grace.

We do not normally allow ourselves to feel shame because we are not sure that we can accept the fact of what we are ashamed of as part of who we are. Although we may be very egocentric, we do not really love ourselves very much. We are extremely unforgiving towards ourselves, and even more so of petty weakness than of great crimes. Therefore, we are most unwilling to disfigure our carefully constructed ideal self with any "unacceptable traits." We fear the loss of love, even our own. Since we do not love the weakness which is in us, we also assume that no one else can either—and certainly not God. In fact, we secretly feel that we always have to appear "at our best" before God. To experience shame in the presence of God then, while it might not at first seem to constitute what we would like to call grace, is in fact just that—grace—for it liberates us. We discover that not only do we not hate ourselves in our new self-knowledge, but also that God does not hate us. Only this kind of experience can persuade us that we are genuinely loved *as we are*, and not as we believe we ought to be or try to pretend we are.

And so, one day I saw myself as tattered, grimy, and bedraggled—a spiritual orphan child who would rather stay angry than ask for the grace to be patient. In this wretched condition, I watched myself crumple down onto the ground, hiding my face in my hands. I could not, would not look at the glorious Trinity before me in beautiful, brilliant, radiant light. A dark heap, I crouched despairingly before Father, Son, and Spirit and said, "How can You look at me like this?" And heard God answer, "You are my friend and I love you." Also: "The darkness is as light to Me." Finally, I raised my eyes and said, "I only want to look at You." Slowly I stood up, still all grimy and tattered. I looked at the Lord who was looking at me. In the presence of all that brilliance, only God's Light was there to be seen, and not my darkness.

Living Waters

The first grace of shame and confusion (however reluctantly prayed for) having been granted, brings about a beginning of freedom and a possibility for more honest communication. Both parties to the dialogue now have access to previously restricted territory. The next Exercises of the first week begin with a petition for the grace of "great and intense sorrow and tears for my sins." While sorrow is perhaps a more expected response to meditations on sin (because it is more traditional), it is unlikely that it could ever really emerge without the interior opening up brought about by the first grace (shame and confusion). Genuine contrition cannot be contrived or produced by will power. It comes as gift, and most spontaneously to the one who has been opened by and to the action of the Holy Spirit.

Real contrition is an attitude relative to God, not to people or circumstances. One can be sorry, for instance, for losing one's temper, for being out of control in general. One may see the destructive nature of inconsistent behavior on the lives of other persons, and one may regret bitterly not being a naturally wonderful and ever-patient parent, spouse, co-worker, or friend. These are useful feelings and cause us to struggle more perseveringly towards developing the virtues of patience, gentleness, and especially a sense of humor—all of which are very helpful for human relationships of any kind. Such feelings are not what one would properly call contrition, however. Fortunately for us, God is very willing to be identified with us creatures, so much so that when Jesus describes the final judgment, the King (also a shepherd) will regard all good and evil done "to the least ones" as having been done to him personally:

> For I was hungry and you gave me food, I was thirsty and you gave me drink, a stranger and you welcomed me, naked and you clothed me, ill and you cared for me, in prison and you visited me.... Amen, I say to you, whatever you did for one of these least brothers of mine, you did for me (Matt. 25:35-36, 40).

And so it is possible to be encouraged that any puny attempts at goodness to others will be held by the Lord as effort on his behalf, and that remorse and frustration over our failures in loving will also contain something of sorrow for sin.

When, however, we are pierced by sorrow because we have received the grace to see our own sinfulness against the horizon of the Infinity of God, something different happens. This is no longer an experience in which the powers of reason and will can be applied first to judge the consequences of our actions and then to resolve to amend them. Rather, it is a gift which alters from within—instantly, deeply, and wholly mysteriously. Above all, it is not an experience of agonizing remorse but rather one of unimaginable love. To describe the differences among these various modes of spiritual growth, let us borrow an image from the *Life* of Teresa of Avila. She compares the soul's growth to the cultivation of a garden, the blossoming of which will give pleasure to the Lord. There is need for water, however, and this may be supplied in a variety of ways: it may be drawn from a well, moved by means of a water wheel and aqueducts, or brought from a river or stream. These methods require successively less work on the part of the gardener. But the finest means of irrigation is the rainfall, where the Lord waters the garden without any help at all from the gardener.[4] While Teresa's watering image refers to prayer in general, in terms of the labor of the person praying and the spontaneous gift of God, it is particularly apt in the present context, I think, because the topic is tears.

What of those tears which are the second constituent of this grace to be prayed for? They too cannot be contrived. Can they be considered a gift for our technological age? Ignatius himself wept frequently and intensely, and reports in his *Spiritual Journal* such protracted episodes of copious tears, occasionally accompanied by sobbing, that he even feared for his eyesight.[5] The history of Christian spirituality is, one might say, watered with the tears of the saints. Weeping was viewed as an important moment of prayer as early as the fourth century when hermits and the first monks were seeking holiness in the Egyptian desert.

The tears Ignatius instructs one to pray for are, in fact, a rain which waters the desert of the heart, softening the crusty soil and making it permeable to grace. Once I imagined that I was dying. I sat on the sofa in my living room, but saw myself as a frail old woman lying in bed with a few dear friends and family members around me. I could see very clearly how I looked. My hair was white. My whole body was very thin and had become almost too weak to move. I looked at my hands, lying motionless on the bedclothes, and at my face. I was visibly withering, my skin dry and like parchment—or like dead leaves which the least wind could waft away. It seemed that there was very little substance left to me.

I knew that I was dying, but was not in pain. Nor was I agitated or afraid. What I felt was inexpressible grief. And I wept, as I sat there on my living room sofa, real tears for my dying self and for the loss of these loved ones who had gathered near me. Then I looked up and could see, through the picture window, my beloved flower and vegetable garden, now covered with January snow. The sun was brilliant on the snowy yard and also in the room where I sat. And the tears, which had begun at the thought of leaving my human companions, now doubled or tripled in volume as I realized that I must part from the earth: from the garden, and the changing seasons, and the sunlight on snow. I mourned them as I have never mourned any loss in all my life. Or perhaps it was that in them I mourned all the losses of my life.

Finally I turned the eyes of my dying self towards God. Nor can I explain just how this was. But in the moment of seeing God before me, who was to my eyes astonishing and unspeakable goodness and love, I also saw, as it were, behind me, all my past sins. These I could not see in their particularity and detail, but as some dark collective mass. In my awareness of them, and while I still looked towards God in wonderment and joy, the enormity of the love and the sorrow of that moment poured from my eyes in an ever greater stream of tears. My feelings were very simple: there was no hope, no fear, no remembrance of the past nor thought of the future. In that moment, all I knew was love and sorrow, and all I saw was the beauty of God over against the dark lump of my sin.

When I had ceased weeping, I felt only peace. Never before nor since have I ever experienced that sort of contrition. And though I may pray for the grace to know it again before or at the hour of my death, I think that in some way that was, in fact, the hour of my death and my tears a gift given "out of time" for that very hour.

The question remains: why tears? I only know that there are things which the soul wants and needs to speak, for which there is no discursive language. The tears which are shed in such moments are true envoys of the heart and speak "words" of "love, joy, peace, patience, kindness, generosity, faithfulness, gentleness, self-control" (Gal. 5:22-23), which have been planted in the heart by the indwelling Trinity. St. Catherine of Siena, who includes a whole chapter on tears in her famous spiritual treatise, *The Dialogue*, sees the gift of tears as part of the prayer of the Spirit within us described by St. Paul in the Letter to the Romans. God speaks to her thus:

> ...you will see that the Holy Spirit weeps in the person of every one of my servants who offers me the fragrance of holy desire and constant humble prayer. This, it seems, is what the glorious apostle Paul meant when he said that the Holy Spirit weeps before me, the, Father "with unspeakable groaning" for you.[6]

Discerning the Spirits

Tears are one of a variety of indices which Ignatius uses for evaluating the movements of the heart towards God, and to which he gives the name "spiritual consolation." This he defines in an appendix of rules for the discernment of spirits:

> I call it consolation when some interior movement in the soul is caused, through which the soul comes to be inflamed with love of its Creator and Lord.... Likewise, when it sheds tears that move to love of its Lord.... Finally, I call consolation every increase of hope, faith, and charity, and all interior joy which calls and attracts

to heavenly things and to the salvation of one's soul, quieting it and giving it peace in its Creator and Lord. [316]

The last statement is the most important in this definition. The final criterion of consolation is not so much the specific feeling or response we may notice, as the result it produces: any increase in faith, hope, love, joy, and peace. Thus, what is significant is not whether we weep or not, for instance, but whether this experience produces greater love in us.

There is, of course, also an experience of spiritual desolation, producing in us the opposite effects of consolation, i.e., turmoil, confusion, and a lack of faith, hope, love, and joy. These experiences of desolation and consolation occur throughout life, and not just in the course of doing the Exercises. What Ignatius provides is a tool for responding creatively to the various movements, so that one need not be simply a passive victim of them, but may use them diagnostically, and avoid being over-whelmed by feelings.

Without personally examining the ontology of the various "spirits" responsible for our states of desolation and consolation, one can, nonetheless, profit greatly from observing those inner conditions themselves. Ignatius defined desolation as follows:

I call desolation all the contrary of the third rule [on consolation], such as darkness of soul, disturbance in it, movement to things low and earthly, the unquiet of different agitations and temptations, moving to want of confidence, without hope, when one finds oneself all lazy, tepid, sad, and as if separated from [one's] Creator and Lord. [317]

Certainly, this sad state can well apply when one has begun seriously the meditations of the first week. It is in a moment such as this that reflection on the "Principle and Foundation" can be very illuminating. In fact, the story of my mountain walk in Colorado (described in the first chapter) can well illustrate the alternation of desolation and consolation in the course of one afternoon. As I started out, I was disoriented, confused, frustrated, "as if separated from [my] Creator and Lord." Eventually my lack of faith, hope, and love gave way to great love, deep peace, thankfulness, and a knowledge of the presence of my Creator and Lord. The memory of this "principle and foundation" is very powerful and can uphold me in a time of desolation, even though I am wholly unable to recreate it experientially for myself. I cannot feel how it *felt*, but I *know* that it was.

During the Exercises of the first week one becomes, in fact, quite open to the "spirits" which produce both consolation and desolation, including the possibility of dark hopelessness at the prospect of sin and its consequences. One evening, for instance, I partied with friends until quite late, and had a wonderful time. But I had to face the next morning after a night of too little sleep and too much food and wine. To make matters worse, I was doing the fifth Exercise (on hell), painfully conscious of my queasy stomach, fuzz-filled head, and heavy eyelids. I could barely concentrate. My groggy physical condition felt like a layer of insulation. Not only did I feel separate from God—I was also out of touch with my own mind and heart. The time passed in a distracted and unfocused way. I found myself watching the clock, very tempted to put an end to this agony which I would not choose to label prayer.

Towards the end of the time, and very surprisingly to me, my feelings changed. I did in fact desire to pray, to be no longer separate from God. I imagined Jesus to be in a favorite place where I have found him in the past, standing in a shallow stream. The water is beautifully clear with smooth, rounded stones on the bottom. It sparkles as it flows over the stones which are variously colored in the sunlight. I stayed on the shore and found that I was praying for myself—for help, for mercy.

In the course of this time, I had become intensely aware of the times of alienation in my life, of sin, of separation—in a word, of my own particular moments of hell. The meditation was no longer an exercise; it was an experienced reality. I had, at one time or another, broken many commandments, failed in many virtues. Now in my (still) foggy and hungover condition, I perceived that none of those things for which I had deliberately left the presence of God could really satisfy me. None of them filled the void within me. I discovered my need and longing for God and, amazingly, I wanted to continue to feel this need, like hunger. I did not wish anything to dull this particular longing.

This story is one of both desolation and consolation. It describes a change which cannot be ascribed to anything I might have done. Nor can it be explained by any external changes in my circumstances. I felt as physically ill when I was finished as I had at first. Grace, unearned and unexpected, was given at a moment of great weakness, when I had felt neither hope nor courage, neither faith nor love. This was not at all a pleasurable experience but it was, in the Ignatian sense, a consoling one, for its end was faith, hope, and love.

Waiting for Grace

Soul of Christ, sanctify me.
Body of Christ, save me.
Blood of Christ, inebriate me.
Water from the side of Christ, wash me.
Passion of Christ, strengthen me.
O good Jesus, hear me;
Within thy wounds hide me;
Suffer me not to be separated from thee;
From the malignant enemy defend me;
In the hour of my death call me,
And bid me come to thee,
That with thy saints I may praise thee
Forever and ever. Amen.   (*Anima Christi*)

Desolation does not always pass so easily from one hour to the next. One might find oneself in desolate distress for a good long time. This can be very painful and discouraging. Inevitably, the temptation which presents itself during a time of desolation is to escape from the experience of it. We do not feel enthusiastic about prayer and so tend to shorten the time given to it, or even avoid praying altogether. Furthermore, we do not wish to reflect upon our awkward condition and so often plunge into distracting activities: shopping sprees, intensive work, a full social calendar. And we have recourse to all sorts of addictions: eating, drinking, playing bridge.

All of these "natural" responses to desolation are exactly the opposite of what Ignatius has to recommend, however. While he advises against making any changes in our *choices* during desolation, he does recommend that we change *ourselves*. Since desolation is a movement which guides us away from God and causes us to experience a decrease in faith, hope, and love, we are to fight it intensely. The means at our disposal are prayer, meditation, self-examination, and penance. None of these means seem very attractive when one is already desolate, but Ignatius insists upon great generosity on the part of the person doing the Exercises.

The state of desolation is, in itself, very illuminating and may be, therefore, full of grace. Catherine of Siena sees it as a place of genuine self-knowledge: ". . . at no time does the soul know herself so well . . . as when she is most beleaguered!"[7] Prayer in the midst of such desolation can feel sometimes like agony.

Packing one's worldly goods and preparing to move to a new place is one such experience. When our family did this, we spent a month surrounded by cardboard cartons and unhung curtains. During this time my prayers were often dominated by feelings of guilt, anger, and hopelessness at my inability to create an orderly cosmos around me (the discovery that I was not God, but a most finite creature indeed). In my distress, I could not concentrate. I could not pray. I was distracted and impatient. I felt angry with God for this state of desolation. I had come to deep knowledge of the disorder in my life, past and present, but blamed God for expecting the impossible—that I might ever change. I felt abandoned in my own darkness, surrounded by dislocated objects to which I, alas, was very attached. In time, a glimmer of light pierced through my inner storm. It was as if God were saying, "I have not abandoned you. But I want you to know the depth of your helplessness, so that you will also know your need for me."

Bereft of the feelings of intense joy and love resulting from spiritual consolation, one has an opportunity to discover real ambivalence, apathy, weakness, lack of perseverance, and frailty in general. We learn how absolutely we rely upon God and the overwhelming support of grace. In the moment of truth which is humility, we come before God and acknowledge from barren hearts our poverty. Out of such awareness, as from a protracted and difficult labor, comes the birth of a purified way of loving.

To the one who remains, in faith, through the anguish of long desolation, this darkness will yield in one way or another to the light which is the knowledge of God. Specifically, in the first week of the *Spiritual Exercises*, the chaos of guilt, confusion, anxiety, and turmoil which may accompany the meditations on sin will also give way to a most peaceful acceptance. This is a realistic self-acceptance which can take place because of the slowly dawning trust that God does, in fact, accept and love us *as we are*, in all our fragmentation and sinfulness. It is an acceptance which allows us to say with real conviction that we are sinners who know in our lives the saving impulse of grace. This is quite a different statement from the one most commonly made (unconsciously) that we are by nature good persons who occasionally (and, of course, atypically) act under the impulse of evil. While the latter statement claiming basic wholeness places us under an intolerable burden of appearing equal to it, the first statement of our sinfulness arouses in us freedom, and amazing thankfulness.

The progress towards such liberating acceptance is slow, however, and at times quite hard to distinguish. The "means" for dealing with desolation, which Ignatius suggests, serve us then as ways of staying on a straight course during a very foggy and tumultuous night voyage. In a sense, the attention to prayer and penance may be the only indicator of our desire to be faithful and to grow in love, at a time when all our feelings suggest that we are hopelessly unfaithful and know nothing at all about love. Our prayer and penance become a promise of waiting, a concrete way of showing our willingness to let God work in us that which is, in fact, impossible—our conversion (which is, in any case, not a one-time event, but a life-long project). It is a time of waiting for grace, to be sure, and yet the very fact of our waiting is an indication that the Lord of all grace is already present.

The waiting referre͏   iting but, in fact, very active. W͏l   l light are totally at the disposal   , it is still appropriate to fight t   rom God with all the means at   : means is prayer—insistent, int   f the spe- cific techniques whicl   prayer of the Exercises is the "t͏.

In the third Exercise of the first week, he instructs the praying person to address first Mary, then Jesus, and finally the Father. These conversations have a specific structure connected with the petition for the grace associated with the Exercise. In this case, the grace itself has a threefold nature: 1) knowledge of and hatred for sin; 2) knowledge of and hatred for the disorder of one's life, so that it may be corrected; and 3) knowledge of and hatred for those things which turn one's life away from Christ. The process, as Ignatius outlines it, has the person pray first that Mary intercede with God on his/her behalf regarding this grace. One concludes with a "Hail Mary." Then one addresses Christ as mediator with the Father and closes this part of the colloquy with the prayer "Soul of Christ" (the traditional *Anima Christi* with which this section began, a favorite prayer of St. Ignatius). Finally, one speaks one's petition directly to God the Father and concludes the entire meditation with an "Our Father."

What is the rationale and function of such a complex prayer structure? There is clearly an increase of intensity in this triple presentation of a petition. In the same way that the repetitions of the Exercises themselves allow them to be entered into at an increasingly deep and intense level, the repeated petitions for grace work towards producing an ever stronger desire for that grace and a genuine act of petition. One is led then to want, ask, and beg for the grace one needs. We often ask for God's gifts rather perfunctorily, without seriously considering whether we really want them. Within the confines of our usual protective shell of pride and self-reliance, we lack the sense of our absolute dependence upon God, until we actually beg for grace and come to know the totality of our need.

There is another facet to these colloquies which is helpful to the person praying. We petition God the Father, asking first the mediation of Mary and Christ (or we may, in fact, seek the intercession of any or all of the saints). On this subject, an anecdote recorded by Karl Rahner in an essay on prayer to the saints may be illuminating:

> When I was in Rome during the Council, I had the opportunity, together with a group of others, to meet the great Protestant theologian Karl Barth. Our discussion turned to the veneration of the Virgin. I asked Karl Barth whether an individual may ask another Christian to pray for him. After a short hesitation, he replied that the individual should ask his fellow Christian to pray *with* him.[8]

In the colloquies, it becomes clear that we do not stand alone before God when we pray. The reality of the communion of saints and of the presence of the "great high Priest" interceding for us impresses itself upon us. In the context of this experienced companionship of those who love us and pray for us, our prayer becomes, of necessity, more truthful, more humble.

In his book, *Radical Prayer*, David J. Hassel, S.J., presents a creative variation on the threefold colloquy which he calls the "Triple Trip." In this exercise, one literally travels first to some place associated with Mary, where one has personally known her presence, companionship, or influence. (If such a trip were not physically possible, I should think an imaginative journey might be almost as useful.) At "Mary's Place," one simply asks her, "How do I stand before you, Mary?" and then waits quietly and patiently for a response. As Hassel points out, whether one is met with a clear answer or with silence, this is a prayer of mutual presence and trust. The second part of the trip is made to Jesus (wherever one is accustomed to meet him), in the company of Mary. One asks of Jesus, "How, Lord, do I stand before you?" In this encounter, Mary may take part in the conversation. Again, the important work of the person praying is to wait and listen. I need to hear what Jesus and Mary have to say to each other about me. Finally, in the company of both Jesus and Mary, one walks or drives to some place associated in one's life with the Father. Again one is to wait and listen as Mary and Jesus enter into the conversation as one's friends and intercessors. One asks here, "Father, how do I stand before you?" Again there is time to wait, listen, trust. This whole exercise is then closed with an "Our Father."[9]

What is particularly helpful about such an exercise, as Hassel describes it, is the realization that, although based on a form called "colloquy," it is not a very wordy affair. We may speak to Jesus, Mary, and the Father. They may address us in very particular ways. The entire time may also be spent, however, in the silent companionship we experience in the presence of those we know and love. True friendship, real love, and genuine prayer do not require the exchange of many words. The act of physically going to three different places in the exercise is itself a part of the prayer—a concrete expression of the desire to be in the presence of Jesus, Mary, and the Father. Like kneeling or other gestures of reverence, it is a means of worshipping with the body as well as with the mind and heart.

The colloquies may well take place in and through our Scriptural readings and contemplations themselves, and need not be seen as a "closing remark" reserved for the last fifteen minutes of prayer. The friendship of Mary, Christ, or the Father can guide us through our prayer. In this case, the colloquy has the nature of a simple mutual presence, superimposed upon or underlying our more discursive meditations.

I was reading the First Letter of John, for instance. It had seemed to me at first rather depressing. All I could hear were words of darkness:

> If we say, "We have fellowship with him," while we continue to walk in darkness, we lie and do not act in truth.... If we say, "We are without sin," we deceive ourselves, and the truth is not in us.... If we say, "We have not sinned," we make him a liar and his word is not in us (1 John 1:6, 8, 10).

And yet this particular Letter is actually full of light, hope, and the promise of forgiveness. Gradually, as I continued to read, I found myself drawn more and more into the words of this piece of Scripture, and also deeply aware of the presence of Mary who was, as it were, accompanying me through the text.

The very words now affected me in a wholly different way. I began to see for the first time the forgiveness of which the Letter speaks:

> But if anyone does sin, we have an Advocate with the Father, Jesus Christ the righteous one (1 John 2:1).

The Letter speaks of the light which comes to cast out the darkness of sin. As I read these verses, I felt as though I were literally walking along the words themselves, making a journey, and seeing for the first time the landscape of the text as it really was. The presence of Mary on that walk in some way opened my eyes and ears to the words I was traversing.

Eventually, it seemed that Mary had led me into the presence of Jesus, in whose company I continued my reading of the Letter. Now I read:

> Beloved, I am writing no new commandment to you but an old commandment that you had from the beginning. The old commandment is the word that you have heard. And yet I do write a new commandment to you, which holds true in him and among you, for the darkness is passing away, and the true light is already shining (1 John 2:7-8).

The words were now filled with love and light and led me back to even more ancient words:

> Hear, O Israel! The LORD is our God, the LORD alone! Therefore, you shall love the LORD, your God, with all your heart, and with all your soul, and with all your strength. Take to heart these words which I enjoin on you today. Drill them into your children. Speak of them

at home and abroad, whether you are busy or at rest. Bind them at your wrist as a sign and let them be as a pendant on your forehead. Write them on the doorposts of your houses and on your gates.
(Deut. 6:4-9)

The Hebrew Scriptures give us a great sense of the power of the word, both for good and for evil. The word of God, the words of these texts, are a living reality with the power to give life. More and more, the words themselves receded in my mind before the simple awareness of the Word, Christ, in whose presence I was held.

After a while, I found that Jesus had indeed led me before the Father, with whom I very slowly continued the "journey" through the second chapter of 1 John. My awareness was filled with the knowledge of the forgiving love of God which had become, in the course of this exercise, a real event for me and not merely an intellectual understanding of a passage of Scripture. Resting upon the breast of the Father, I *was* a child, fed and wrapped in love, speechless, trembling, and full of thanksgiving. Slowly I spoke words: "Our Father, . . . hallowed be thy name. . . ." The syllables stretched into infinity, barely breathed in joy, fear, and utter silence.

Notes

[1]*Encounters with Silence*, (Westminster, Maryland: Newman Press, 1965), p. 13.

[2]From *The Collected Works of St. Teresa of Avila, Volume I*, translated by Kieran Kavanaugh and Otilio Rodriguez (Copyright 1976 by Washington Province of Discalced Carmelites, ICS Publications, 2131 Lincoln Rd, NE, Washington, DC 20002, USA), p. 213.

[3]Roland Barthes, who in his remarkable *Sade, Fourier, Loyola* deals not at all with the substance of Ignatius' work, sees as its unique contribution the development of a language with which one might address and elicit a response from God. New York: Hill and Wang, 1976, pp. 38-75.

[4]*Collected Works*, vol. 1, 81.

[5]*Spiritual Diary*, #107, in Antonio T. de Nicolas, *Powers of Imagining: Ignatius de Loyola*, (Albany: State University of New York, 1986), p. 208.

[6]*The Dialogue*, trans. Suzanne Noffke, O.P., (New York: Paulist Press, 1980), p. 169.

[7]*The Dialogue*, p. 168.

[8]"Prayer to the Saints" in Karl Rahner and Johann B. Metz, *The Courage to Pray*, (New York: Crossroad, 1981), p. 70.

[9]David J. Hassel, S.J., *Radical Prayer*, (New York: Paulist Press, 1983), pp. 52-54.

Chapter Three
Reconciliation

Penance: A Practical Guide

In the course of the *Spiritual Exercises*, and especially during the first week and in times of desolation, Ignatius encourages the practice of penance. He takes care to point out that penance is both an external act and an internal orientation—sorrow for sin and a return to the love and service of God. He then lists three specific areas of penance: as regards food, sleep, and "other kinds of austerity."

Penance regarding eating and sleeping is easy to define: one does less of them. In terms of the Exercises, sleep may well be curtailed in order to find more solitary time for prayer. This is especially true for anyone living in a family. Fasting may take many forms and should be suited to the demands of a person's work and community responsibilities. One should not become exhausted from lack of proper rest and nourishment, but if one is not somewhat uncomfortable, one can hardly claim to be doing penance. If our penance seems difficult and unenjoyable, if we suddenly crave chocolate layer cake, and if in our struggle to resist such a temptation we begin to see ourselves as weak-willed, in need of help, and surprisingly attached to our creature comforts, so much the better. We need to know our lack of freedom and our divided loyalties.

Being determined to skip lunch one Saturday, I was distressed to witness my husband preparing a toasted cheese sandwich for himself. Swiss cheese and rye bread suddenly seemed like manna in the desert. Like Esau, I would gladly have traded my birthright for the satisfaction of my hunger (which was by no means dire, since I had eaten breakfast). I fled to the basement where the weekly laundry was in process and, leaning on the washing machine while tears filled my eyes, I spontaneously prayed, "Help, Lord! I'm doing this because I love you and want to be like you." Until those words emerged from my lips, I did not even know they were true. It was a moment of knowing my own frailty, and a moment of seeing the disproportionate relationship between my desire to follow Christ and my desire for a cheese sandwich. A function of penance which Ignatius does not mention is that it shows us our true selves, gives us knowledge of our dependencies, and stimulates a salutary sense of humor.

As for the third category of penance mentioned in the Exercises, I have no personal knowledge of the kinds of bodily penances practiced by the saints or by members of monastic communities. I do not even know where one might acquire a hair shirt in twentieth-century America! It seems to me, however, that the best penance for anyone is not the extraordinary and heroic, but something quite common and appropriate to one's particular circumstances. This is especially humbling because of its ordinariness. One does not choose such penance as a grand gesture, but does it simply, quietly, and as a service to one's community. I always find a special grace in the "penance" of scrubbing floors (whether because of the symbol of cleansing waters or because of the necessity to go down upon one's knees, I do not know).

The domestic service of one's immediate family or community provides a variety of opportunities for penance if one will but use one's imagination. (This suggestion is not intended only or even primarily for women, many of whom have lived from childhood in the concept that domestic service of others constitutes their only identity. Fasting is only appropriate for those who have enough to eat—not for the starving.) The point of any form of mortification or self-denial is not to prove that I am a successful and stoical ascetic. Penance is not an end in itself but a means to the end towards which I direct my entire life: the love of God and of God's creation.

Penance should contribute towards moving the needs and pleasures of others to the center of my consciousness, and my own needs and pleasures to the periphery. Often the simplest things can be the most effective. For instance, a parent may not find it extraordinary to get up during the night for a sick child, but suffer intensely when asked to play yet one more game of "Monopoly" on a rainy afternoon. We like to think of ourselves as heroes. Being a servant is much harder. A further benefit of simple "domestic" penances is that they tend not to reinforce pride and a sense of accomplishment. Rather our self-importance may diminish as we cultivate some genuine patience and a healthy ability to laugh at ourselves.

In a mysterious way, acts of penance, perhaps because they redirect the focus of our attention away from ourselves and towards God and our neighbor, become acts of love. In the course of the first week of the *Spiritual Exercises*, one may do penance while in the turmoil and confusion of desolation that often accompanies a deeper knowledge of one's own sin. Such penance is then a bodily prayer of waiting for grace: the grace of sorrow, of acceptance of oneself as sinner and of God as forgiving, and the grace of conversion.

During the first week, these graces, for which one has begged, may come to gradually replace the movements of desolation, leaving a deep peace and thankfulness. It is almost paradoxical that the new and profound self-knowledge and awareness of sin which ensues from the meditations of the first week should be accompanied by intense gratitude and love for the God whom we have encountered in these exercises on sin. Indeed it is only in the context of knowing ourselves as saved and redeemed that we have been able to come to an awareness of sin at all. This experience may, in turn, lead us to desire to do penance—no longer now as a way of asking and waiting for the grace of sorrow, but as a real expression of that sorrow, as an act of love.

The images in Psalm 137 are very beautiful. The people of Israel weep and do not sing in the place of their exile. They view their expulsion from the promised land, God's land, as an exile in fact from God:

By the streams of Babylon
  we sat and wept
  when we remembered Zion.
On the aspens of that land
  we hung up our harps. . . .
How could we sing a song of the Lord
  in a foreign land? (Ps. 137:1-2, 4).

When I read this psalm in the context of the first week, I thought of the exile of Israel as the alienation from God that is sin and hell.

As I thought of the exiled people weeping by the streams, I also thought of the divine shepherd of Psalm 23 who leads the sheep "beside restful waters," and of the times in the Gospels when Jesus presents himself as the good shepherd. I saw myself returning to his sheepfold, wishing to end my exile, to be no longer among the lost. I said, "Lord I want to be one of yours—not lost, not exiled—only one of yours." And when Jesus stretched out his hand to lead me in, I said, "Just let me stay here at the gate to mourn and do penance." Then, with a look full of the amused tolerance of love, he said, "You can do that if you like, but come inside first." I felt at home and grateful, and I laughed. It is important to see the relationship between the Light and lightness. We must not sentimentalize our relationship with the Lord. Grace gives us a certain levity which is truly an antidote to the gravity of sin.

The Celebration of Passover

Ignatius makes the assumption that the person progressing through the first week of the *Spiritual Exercises* will wish to make a general confession and it is, in fact, traditional to do so. Ignatius himself records in his autobiography having made such a confession, the preparation for which (in writing) took him three days.[1] In an age when sacramental confession is neither so frequently nor universally practiced among Catholics, and is not formally recognized at all in many Christian churches, the notion of making a confession covering one's entire life history might seem indeed daunting. After entering deeply (and at times painfully) into the Exercises of the first week, however, one does not remain in the turmoil of the initial confrontations with one's sinful self. There is a passage into joyful acceptance of one's own finitude and thankfulness for God's forgiveness. One may truly desire to celebrate this reconciliation sacramentally, in a formal or informal way.

The Exercises of the first week had drawn me to notice more and more the power of words in my life, both as carriers of grace and as weapons of sin and darkness. I had also come to know the life-giving reality of God's word:

> So shall my word be
> that goes forth from my mouth;
> It shall not return to me void,
> but shall do my will,
> achieving the end for which I sent it (Is. 55:11).

It had now become necessary to express sorrow and repentance, as well as love and thanksgiving, *in words*. And so, on Holy Thursday, I met with my confessor-friend to celebrate these events. While I had a general sense of what I needed to say, I had not prepared a detailed "script" for this confession. It seemed important to leave some windows open for the entrance of the Holy Spirit.

It was very surprising to hear myself saying, at the very beginning, "Until I was about eleven years old, I loved God." What followed was a narration, in terms of the educational, professional, and personal milestones in my life, of many infidelities regarding that love. For about forty-five minutes I spoke words, and then there was no more to say. In fact, I was speechless. So was my listener. We both stood silent upon the holy ground of a human life—my own life—which now appeared as a chapter of salvation history. While I had spoken of sin and darkness, what emerged ever more clearly, through all the meanderings of my tale, was the amazing presence of grace and light in it. It was a story of the Exodus, of a passover from death into life, from bondage into freedom.

St. Paul's statement in Romans that ". . . where sin increased, grace overflowed all the more" (Rom. 5:20), was a reality of which I had now become conscious. The presence of God in the events of my life had become as visible as the pillar of cloud and the pillar of fire which had led the Hebrew people out of Egypt. In spite of all rebellions and murmurings in the desert of my personal salvation history, the fidelity of God had been absolute. At the end, there were none of my own words remaining, only the words of God's forgiving love. And so, it is right to give thanks and praise.

Note

[1]"Autobiography," #17, in *Powers of Imagining*, p. 255.

Chapter Four
Mission and Discipleship: The "Second Week"

The Call of the King

In the "second week" of the *Spiritual Exercises*, Ignatius turns his attention to the life of Jesus. In doing these Exercises, we are meant also to attend to our own life stories and to see the points where they intersect with the mission of Christ. The acceptance and gratitude, which have sprung from the experience of love and forgiveness in the first week, have brought us to a place from which we can look out and survey the various landscapes of the Gospels, of human history, and of our own experience.

More than any other part of the *Exercises*, this week bears upon the matter of choice. It is the time of making elections: of choosing permanent or temporary paths, of re-evaluating and perhaps modifying old ones, of reinforcing and affirming primary commitments. To open the two-pronged movement of this second week (a deep contemplation of the events of the life of Jesus, and the directing or redirecting of our own hearts and lives into his service), Ignatius presents the important contemplation on the Kingdom.

In his text, Ignatius builds upon the loyalty of a subject to a good king who proposes to conquer all enemies and create a Christian commonwealth. To Ignatius, who knew the life of a soldier and the loyalty and dedication which might be instilled by a leader worthy of trust, the response was self-evident. He asks that one:

> ...consider what the good subjects ought to answer to a king so liberal and so kind, and hence, if anyone did not accept the appeal of such a king, how deserving he would be of being censured by all the world, and held for a mean-spirited knight. [94]

Clearly, a generosity of spirit is presupposed for any further progress in this Exercise.

The second part of the contemplation reflects, on the basis of analogy with our obvious response to a good king, on the much greater loyalty and service to be rendered to Christ the King. Essential to both parts of the meditation is the perfect identity of life and fortunes between the leader and those who follow. Ignatius writes in the person of the good king:

> . . . whoever would like to come with me is to be content to eat as I, and also to drink and dress, etc., as I: likewise he is to labor like me in the day and watch in the night, etc., that so afterwards he may have part with me in the victory, as he had it in the labors. [93]

In the person of Christ the King, he writes: ". . . whoever would like to come with Me is to labor with Me, that following Me in the pain, he [she] may also follow Me in the glory" [96]. For Ignatius, there is no question about the reasonableness of such an association. To follow such a leader is not a matter of faith but of common sense: ". . . all those who have judgment and reason will offer their entire selves to the labor" [97].

What is striking in this Exercise is that Ignatius makes one further point for those who wish to offer more than even this total dedication would imply. He suggests that one pray words such as these:

> . . . I want and desire, and it is my deliberate determination, if only it be for Thy greater service and praise, to imitate Thee in bearing all injuries and all abuse and all poverty of spirit, and actual poverty, too, if Thy most Holy Majesty wants to choose and receive me to such life and state. [98]

With this petition, Ignatius exceeds the demands of common sense, clear to "all those who have judgment and reason." The generosity of the disciples must be such as contradicts nature, so that Ignatius sees them as "acting against their own sensuality" [98], in seeking poverty (spiritual and material), as well as injuries and abuse. The value of these normally repugnant things inheres, however, not in their own intrinsic nature, but in their potential as agents for the imitation of Christ. The grace of the second week, to be sought through all of the meditations, is a more intimate knowledge, a deeper love, and a more perfect following of Jesus. These Exercises represent an undertaking which is by no means for a "mean-spirited knight," but only for those who are willing to risk losing their very selves.

For Ignatius, the vocabulary and imagery associated with kings, knights, military loyalty, and the glory of battle were genuine products of his experience as a soldier and, therefore, constellated powerful symbols which could move his heart and motivate his choices. In a world where the images of war are more likely to reflect the horrors of nuclear destruction, Ignatius' description of the personal courage, sacrifice, and dedication to a military leader may appear meaningless, even offensive. In a society where only an acceptance of pluralism and a genuine celebration of our differences will enable us to love and respect one another, absolute loyalty to a monarch who promises to conquer all enemies may seem equally absurd. What is central to the Exercise is its symbolic force, however, not its literal detail. A generous openness, combined with creative use of the imagination, should allow the life-giving heart of this very powerful Exercise to be equally as effective today as it must have been in the sixteenth century.

When I considered this Exercise, a scene of total disorder passed through my imagination. It was the sort of cultural disintegration one might conceive of as resulting from twentieth century warfare. Qualities of leadership, great vision, and courage would be needed to begin to rebuild a shattered world, to establish a humane and creative society. And such leadership did emerge. Not a renaissance king, but a surprising pair came to mind: a man and a woman. Around them quickly assembled those committed to the hard work of reconstruction. The tasks were diverse. At first the most elementary emergency measures were required: transportation and distribution of food, provision of shelter, basic needs, and medical care. Then there was the task of providing for the future: there were projects of reforestation, reclamation of swamp lands, intensive agriculture, etc. All of culture was in a state of collapse, so that there were sweeping needs to provide for literacy and all forms of education, justice—social, economic, and domestic—and healthy structures of family and community life. People committed themselves to producing music, art, architecture, forms of worship and, in fact, to all that gives beauty to human societies.

Those who answered the summons to join in the great task, which was in a way the realization of a new creation, gave not only their energies and time, but in fact all they had to the common effort. All remaining wealth, clothing, food supplies, books, and other goods were put at the disposal of the whole. And the strong and healthy gladly supported the sick, the elderly, the very young, and the weak. As Ignatius says, that all this should be so was perfectly obvious to "all those who have judgment and reason."

As I dwelt upon the clear necessity to give one's whole self to the building of a good world community, I saw, as if superimposed upon this first part of the contemplation, that Jesus was speaking to great crowds of people gathered on a grassy mountain slope. The task to which he was calling all those listeners, of whom I was one, was the same work—the building of a new creation. But the depth of the relationship and the commitment, as well as the level of identity and intimacy, between the King and the followers was infinitely more profound.

This call did not extend only to the limits of creating a humane and human society, although it encompassed them. Beyond all self-sacrifice for the common good, beyond mere fidelity to a charismatic leader, beyond all common sense even, was the unambiguous desire to love and to imitate a *person* simply because of who that person was. The crowd was hearing such words as:

> Blessed are the poor in spirit,
> for theirs is the kingdom of heaven....

> Blessed are they who hunger and thirst for righteousness,
>   for they will be satisfied. . . .
> Blessed are you when they insult you and persecute you
>   and utter every kind of evil against you [falsely] because of me.
> (Matt. 5:3, 6, 11)

And also these words were heard:

> But to you who hear, I say, love your enemies, do good to those who hate you, bless those who curse you, pray for those who mistreat you. To the person who strikes you on one cheek, offer the other as well. . . . (Luke 6:27-29).

Gradually, yet a third scene passed before my mind, superimposed upon the previous ones. The King was now standing in a little courtyard. It seemed strange that he should be blindfolded. Suddenly he staggered. There were words: "Play the prophet. Which one struck you?" (Luke 22:64). Later he was treated with great contempt, although those who were insulting him had dressed him in a magnificent robe (Luke 23:11). Then there was a large crowd. I could recognize some of those who had been with me on the mountainside. They were shouting violently, but they did not seem to want to rescue the King. After a long while, the crowds slowly thinned out. It became quiet. The King too was very still—and naked. I could read the sign above his head: "This is the King of the Jews" (Luke 23:38). There were two others dying alongside the King. One of them mocked him as the crowds had done. The other spoke softly: "Jesus, remember me when you come into your kingdom" (Luke 23:42).

I looked at the King and listened to these words. I think I spoke. Perhaps it was a mere whisper, an utterance of the heart. Surely my mind would not have consented, my lips never dared to speak such words:

> I want to join you in this work. I want to be with you. Let me accept with you all poverty and abuse which enters my life. Please choose me for this life of praise and service. Call me to be with you in all of this. . . . And, Jesus, remember me when you come into your kingdom.

The Hidden Jesus

The next group of Exercises for the second week has us look towards the early life of Jesus and again ask for the grace to know, love, and follow him better. It is astounding to think that, in spite of life-long familiarity with the Gospel narratives of the birth and life of Jesus in Nazareth, we know him so very little. Perhaps because of the very fact that these stories are so familiar, we have buried the reality of God's presence in history, the living reality of Jesus, behind the wall of theological doctrines and of theater props—the striped bathrobes and tin foil wings which adorn child shepherds and angels around Christmastime. We can even turn the living history of our salvation into figurines—creche scenes of all descriptions—and set it neatly on our tables where it will remain harmless and unconnected with life. I too have my own set of little wooden figures and love it dearly.

There is a danger, however, that I may never look beyond those magi with their wooden camel train, the farm animals, the shepherds, the piously kneeling Mary and Joseph, and the sweet babe with extended arms, that I may stop at the windows and never look through them to life and truth. The urgent need I have, in doing the Exercises of the second week, is to begin to *see* Jesus. That can only happen when I encounter the Gospel as alive, as fresh, as something new and surprising and *human*, as well as divine. I must begin to hear the words of these Scriptures as good *news*. There is no such thing as the same *old* Gospel. I must also learn to see what is really there and not be distracted, even blinded, by what I expect to be there or what art, music, literature, and especially theology have told me is there.

In the very first contemplation on the Incarnation, Ignatius requires a quite strenuous exercise in seeing. There are two kinds of seeing here, and two kinds of subjects for our seeing: the transcendent Infinite and the particular historical. We are asked first to consider the Trinity, itself in an act of contemplation—of the whole of human history in all times and all places. Then we turn our attention to a very small piece of human history, the annunciation to Mary. We look at a single, not particularly spectacular moment in world history, an obscure village, a poor home, an extremely young woman, and an unknown visitor-messenger-angel.

The vision asked of us is of a different sort. We look towards the Trinity and we look towards this homely and mysterious encounter between Mary and the angel. But there is more. We must look at all of the human landscape as well, and not through our own eyes but through God's. We watch the Trinity watching us, as it were, and through an impossible grace we see our world and history as God sees it. A friend of mine describes his experience of this contemplation as an overwhelming sense of the whole of human society—all of it—present to God, a presence which gives birth to his own desire to be present to—not to lose sight of—all those throngs and generations of people in their needs and struggles.

To see, to have even a small glimpse of the world as God sees it, is a transforming gift and a radical act. For it reorients our usual view of things, in which we are, of course, in the center. It places us at once everywhere and nowhere. We are present to and participate in all of human life and history. And yet at the same time we lose ourselves, if only momentarily, and are simply *seeing* (not, for once, self-regarding).

Having, however feebly, trained our eyes on:

> ...the various persons...in such variety, in dress as in actions: some white and others black; some in peace and others in war; some weeping and others laughing; some well, others ill; some being born and others dying, etc. [106],

and also having heard what all these persons are saying and having seen what they are doing, we are asked by Ignatius to focus our vision on Mary and the angel: to see them, to hear what they are saying, and to notice what they are doing. What is really seen in such a contemplation may be quite surprising. To see something is very different from having merely learned it as a fact or an intellectual proposition.

For the very first time, I noticed how young Mary was. My

little wooden nativity Mary is, after all, quite poised and digni-
fied, a mature woman. But the Mary I now saw was a
girl—vibrant, bursting with life and hope, and also very ordinary, quite poor in fact. She was barefoot and lived in a small
and simple house with the rest of her family. When someone
arrived at the door, she graciously welcomed him. The visitor
appeared in a homespun gray traveling cloak, somewhat dusty
from the road. And Mary, with spontaneous hospitality,
brought a bowl of water to wash his feet, and offered him
something to eat.

Imagining this scene, I remembered the story of Abraham of
whom it was also told that he entertained angels. He greeted the
three men who appeared at his house in the heat of the day:

> Let some water be brought, that you may bathe your feet, and then
> rest yourselves under the tree. Now that you have come this close to
> your servant, let me bring you a little food, that you may refresh
> yourselves, and afterward you may go on your way (Gen. 18:4-5).

It is of such graciousness to a stranger that the Letter to the
Hebrews speaks: "Do not neglect hospitality, for through it
some have unknowingly entertained angels" (Heb. 13:2).

In the village girl and the dusty traveler, I had finally seen
Mary and the angel. I realized that the welcome this girl
extended to a stranger and the homely hospitality she provided
for his comfort were one and the same with her simple response
to his mysterious invitation: "I am the servant of the Lord. Let it
be done to me as you say" (Luke 1:38). The welcome to an
unknown guest and the "yes" to God are not separate, but one.

Especially in the meditations on the early life of Jesus and on
Mary's role in it, the reality which strikes me again and again is
the real humanity of these people. Perhaps what we most often
miss in our pious or academic readings of the Gospels is that
Jesus really lived a human life, in a real time and a real place.
Moreover, the places and events we begin to see are ones of
simplicity, poverty, and obscurity—qualities which do not
carry very great value in our culture. Certainly, I had never
found them to be particularly attractive. And now Ignatius was

asking that I notice all the ordinariness of daily life in the stories of Jesus, and then to find God and my own heart's desire in such ordinary poverty and obscurity. It was indeed a new way of seeing.

"And there were shepherds..."

A friend of mine likes to preach a Christmas sermon about the visit of the shepherds to the Holy Family. They were, he says, the dirtiest, the most disreputable, the most uncouth lot in all of rural society in biblical times. They were simple or simple-minded, tattered, smelly, uneducated, and generally "marginal" people. My own meditations on the shepherds seemed hopelessly disconnected, however. My mind would not accept their relevance to an American context and the exercise was threatening to remain a very academic one.

Suddenly, however, there was a change of scene. The idyllic setting, imposed by my experience since childhood of nativity creches (green grass and grazing sheep, shepherds in earth-tone robes, a starlit hillside), yielded in my mind to a much more contemporary vision. I found myself on a subway platform in Boston. The "shepherds" were now a motley group of travelers: bag ladies, drunks, factory workers, students, joggers, panhandlers, businessmen and women, shoppers, noisy children, and street people of all descriptions. A few of them were just the sort of people I generally avoid looking at on the streets and in the subways. But now I was an integral part of this group, in no way distinguished from the others, and certainly not just an observer looking on.

Among us was a certain man whom I recognized. He often rode the same bus as I, and talked very loudly to the bus driver and anyone else willing to listen. He wore baggy trousers, carried a lunch pail, and seemed always to need a shampoo. He had strong views on many subjects, especially politics and public morality. I knew him instantly as he approached our group waiting on the platform, for I had always found his loud conversations and his opinions very embarrassing. Moreover, his vulnerable camaraderie and assumption of relationship (based on the sole foundation of a common bus route) had always struck me as offensive and inappropriate. Now, however, this man, whom I had unconsciously despised and feared for his lack of reserve, was engaged as I was in a common pilgrimage.

We stood together on the subway platform (the bag ladies, the drunks, the workers, the students, the business people, this nameless man, and I) and when the next train pulled into the station, we all crowded on board. I knew we were going to Dorchester (a working-class neighborhood in Boston with much poverty and some new wealth). We all—shepherds—had one intent, to see the new savior who had been born.

We left the subway and walked to the house which was the goal of our journey. It was one of those classic wood-frame triple-deckers which are the hallmark of so many of the older immigrant neighborhoods of Boston. And there we found the holy family. "Mary" was a teen-ager, a mere child—fragile, vulnerable, obviously overwhelmed, but with a serenity not typical at her age. Her child slept in a plastic bassinet. "Joseph" was a laborer, quite exhausted at the end of the day, and now happily enjoying a can of beer. There was a television on in the room. The young family lived with Mary's parents who were also helping to support them. The mother was powerful and dominant—a matriarch with a strong Boston accent. Her husband, also a laborer, sat very quietly in a corner of the room. He wore a tee-shirt and work pants, and had settled into what was obviously his private chair for a little Monday night football.

There was no doubt in my mind. This was exactly what we had come to see. These were the people we wanted to meet. The shepherds, of whom I was one, had found the savior. In this family, ordinary as it seemed, lay our hope of salvation. Filled with awe at the beauty, the holiness, the simplicity of this reality, I fell to my knees and found myself speaking words like a prayer customarily said at communion: "Lord, I am not worthy to enter under your roof. Speak but the word and I shall be healed." After that, there were no more words—only adoration.

At Mary's Place

There is a relationship with Mary which is established or deepened by means of the colloquies in the Exercises of the first week. This relationship develops into a more profound intimacy and acquaintance with a person in the early contemplations of the second week. Through the narratives in Matthew's and Luke's Gospels, it becomes possible to stand with Mary in her places: Nazareth, Bethlehem, Egypt, to visit Elizabeth with her in the Judean hill country, and to witness her travels to the temple at Jerusalem.

In my imaginings, the home of Mary during the Egyptian exile became a one-room cabin in a very dusty city full of travelers and refugees. This cabin was very simple, but not at all miserable. There I found Mary at work and a one year-old Jesus playing on the floor. The most striking aspect of this home was the atmosphere it created. Although it was actually very small, it seemed to be quite spacious because it was almost totally empty. In fact, it was full of space—a space filled only by the presence of the family who lived there. There was no clutter here. I stood in this room with Mary and watched the play of the child. There was nothing else to do. Nor did I want to do or say anything at all. Being there was wholly sufficient and gave a great sense of peace.

After a while a conversation occurred to me—about loneliness. I asked Mary how she could stand the loneliness of this place of exile. She missed her family and all her friends. She missed the hills of Judea where Elizabeth lived. In this dusty Egyptian town, she missed the green of Galilee. When I admitted how afraid I was of being lonely, of finding any empty spaces in my life, Mary said that when she was lonely she sang the psalms in praise of God. Our conversation went on for a while longer, although we did not always speak. Eventually I turned to the psalms, and the two of us sang Psalm 84 together. Its beauty and appropriateness to the moment stunned me:

How lovely is your dwelling place,
O LORD of hosts!

My soul yearns and pines
    for the courts of the LORD.
My heart and my flesh
    cry out for the living God.
Even the sparrow finds a home,
    and the swallow a nest
    in which she puts her young—
Your altars, O LORD of hosts,
    my king and my God! (Ps. 84:2-4).

We sang the ancient verses with a strange and lovely harmony, and even danced a little bit. Mary's place was full of grace.

The One Thing Necessary

In reflecting upon this experience, I later thought how cluttered my own spaces were in contrast with Mary's simple room. The rooms of my house are filled with things. And the rooms of my mind are busy with the things I see in the rooms of my house. And the chambers of my heart are cluttered with cares and anxieties about all the collections which fill my house and my mind. I knew then a deep yearning for the simplicity I had found at Mary's place. In the end, I was also deeply grateful because there had clearly been created in me at least one small uncluttered space where there was room for Mary's cabin and where the play of the child-God could take place. It was in this central realm, defined by poverty, emptiness, and solitude—a space so barren and lowly as to be only described by negative words—that all desires, frustrations, fears, and even guilt gave way to silence and peace.

The clutter—internal and external—continued and continues to fill my life. Perhaps it must. I may choose to live a relatively simpler lifestyle, but if I am to live in human communities at all, I must make peace with the clutter as well. In fact, so did Mary. Only consider how much traveling she seemed to do! These thoughts led me to the home of that other Mary whom Jesus loved, and her sister Martha. I had always imagined that poor Martha, who after all was only doing her job, was treated very shabbily. Now I saw, however, that Jesus does not reprimand her for her concerns, but only for trying to bring Mary's attention away from him. I could see that Mary, who sits at the feet of Jesus and listens to his words, might be my inner room, a place of stillness, obedience, and trust. When Jesus says, "you are anxious and upset about many things," then I am reminded that all of the work, worry, and administration, which can fill my time and occupy my thoughts, are the Martha in me who remains in charge of life's practical needs, and rightly so. She performs the chores which nurture the household. Mary, who listens peacefully within, is a source of life and direction. She must not be dragged forth from the quiet chamber where she is attentive to the Lord.

In spite of the changing moods and tasks of my daily life, Mary became a place where St. Paul's words took on vital reality:

> For I am convinced that neither death, nor life, nor angels, nor principalities, nor present things, nor future things, nor powers, nor height, nor depth, nor any other creature will be able to separate us from the love of God in Christ Jesus our Lord.
>
> (Rom. 8:38-39)

From time to time, I find that Mary needs to remind Martha of that fact. Martha does have a way of taking charge. But it has proven true that the more engaged Martha becomes in the pressures and demands of work and ministry, the more she is in need of the life-giving presence of Mary, the solitary listener.

Now it seems that Mary and Martha have intruded them-selves prematurely into the second week meditations concerned with the infancy and childhood of Jesus. In fact, these two women—love and service—are well placed here. Their home represents, for the adult Jesus, not his ministry but his leisure. They are his friends. He finds with them a place of hospitality and intimacy. If one sees the stories of the hidden Jesus as a model of contemplative life with its simple obscurity and its humble service, then Martha and Mary are part of this model. Their contemplation is not that of hermitage or cloister, but of all the varieties of family where growth is nurtured by the listening heart.

That Martha and Mary seem to epitomize two extremes of the Christian person, the activist and the prayerful, is a perception which haunts many who seriously pursue the Christian life. There is a danger in the polarity of the two positions. The "devout" may be seduced into a state of spiritual anesthesia where they do not feel the pain of the suffering body of Christ in the world around them. The "political" may be subject to contempt and impatience with those less committed, or else they may simply suffer burn-out as a result of bearing the burden of God's work all by themselves. For Martha and Mary to be truly in Christ, they must respect and nurture each other within the individual Christian, within local communities, and within the global Church.

In my own life, the unresolved conflict between prayer and action became apparent in the context of the story in Luke 2:41-52 of the child Jesus in the temple at Jerusalem. Ignatius clearly sees this episode as a way of entering upon the choice or election to be made during the second week. For an examination of the various states of life, he sees the obedience of Jesus to his parents as a model for normal life in family and society, and the visit to the temple as commitment to the "pure service" of God [135]. It seems to me, however, that Ignatius was presenting a set of alternatives which are not necessarily mutually exclusive. My discontent with the dichotomy became evident in the course of the Exercise. I did not know whether I most identified with Jesus in his need to be in God's house, or with Mary in her (very understandable) familial anxiety.

Resisting the assumption that familial commitment precluded the possibility of a share in the mission of Christ, I found my mind wandering far from Luke's narrative. In something like a daydream, I imagined that a good friend said to me, "You should read Isaiah." That seemed an odd suggestion. Should I read the whole book? Gathering my wits together, I struggled to apply my attention to the scene between Jesus and his parents at the temple. But my mind drifted back to its fantasies and the inner voice was more specific this time: "Try chapter 6 of Isaiah." I had no idea what chapter 6 was all about, ignored the suggestion as absurd, and bent my mind to what I thought was the subject at hand: *either* Jesus *or* Mary. Eventually, however, curiosity triumphed and I turned to Isaiah 6. No longer sleepy and distracted, I found myself riveted to the prophet's description of his vision and call. I realized the relationship between the beauty of the temple which Isaiah sees in his vision and the desire of the boy Jesus to be in the house of the Lord. And I remembered the words of the psalm I had sung *with Mary:*

> How lovely is your dwelling place,
>   O LORD of hosts!
> My soul yearns and pines
>   for the courts of the LORD (Ps. 84:2-3).

Returning to the temple at Jerusalem, I now found no bar to my entrance. I asked Jesus to lead me into this temple. He took me by the hand and led me in.

The words of a psalm which I had sung at Mary's place had allowed me to hear, as addressed to me, the call and sending of a prophet. It was a frightening realization, but one which also consoled me: that I was not necessarily excluded from the work of the Kingdom, that Mary's work is not separate from the mission of Jesus. In concrete terms, an American woman and a person living "in the world" might venture beyond this point in the *Spiritual Exercises*—might, in fact, enter into the temple, see the enthroned Lord, hear the song of the six-winged seraphim, and speak the words: "Here I am; send me" (Is. 6:1-8).

Two Standards and Three Types

Before entering upon the contemplations of the public life of Jesus, Ignatius inserts two pivotal meditations into the second week. The point of these two Exercises, indeed of the whole of the *Spiritual Exercises,* is that we will freely and wholeheartedly choose to follow Christ and to turn from anything else that would divert us from that goal. The "two standards" refer to the flags of the opposing armies of Christ and Lucifer, "mortal enemy of our human nature" [136]. Again Ignatius presents his material by means of a military metaphor. However, the importance of this Exercise and the extremely difficult struggle it may entail are well served by the imagery of battle.

The grace to be prayed for in this Exercise is that one may be accepted to serve Christ under his standard. This seems an obvious and easy choice, until Ignatius sets forth the rigors implied in making it:

> . . . there are to be three steps: the first, poverty against riches; the second, contumely and contempt against worldly honor; the third, humility against pride. [146]

If the means by which the enemy lures men and women to destruction are riches, which lead to honor, which leads to pride, then Ignatius would have us beg for the highest spiritual poverty (and material poverty as well, if God so wills it), which most often leads to insults and contempt, which in turn lead to the humility of Christ. In short, we ask for the grace to share in the fate of the person we profess to follow.

The Exercise on the three types of person is complementary to the two standards. While in the former, attention was focussed "from above" on the ways in which Christ leads men and women, here we have the battle as waged "from below": three human approaches to salvation. The first type would like to be free of attachments which threaten peace and salvation, but these persons do nothing about it. The second type has the same desire, but is only able to compromise. These are the ones who wish to serve God and yet retain their other allegiances. The third group is able to free itself, desiring nothing except that their lives be at the disposal of God's will. They have, in fact, become indifferent to their possessions (both material and non-material) in the Ignatian sense, free "to take the thing or leave it" [155]. The prayer of this Exercise (in the form of the three colloquies) is the same as that for the two standards: that we may serve Christ in poverty, contempt, and humility.

No one who has seriously engaged in these Exercises would deny that they can assume the nature of a battle. Culture, education, and ego-centric inclinations generally view poverty and contempt with some abhorrence. As for humility, it is a misunderstood and undervalued virtue in modern culture. Indeed, Ignatius anticipates a struggle and suggests an antidote. He adds a note that when we discover in ourselves a repugnance for poverty, we beg for it all the more insistently! This procedure should presumably tip the balance in the direction of our disinclinations, thus rendering us indifferent, freer, more disposable.

To say that my encounter with these Exercises was marked by resistance would be a severe understatement. My initial reaction to them was fury! I said, "How dare Ignatius write such things!" For him the highest spiritual poverty meant being an apostle, leading others to Christ. For me it meant moving to where I did not want to go, leaving a place where I wanted to be, leaving friends and support, not having a job, being insecure about my present and future vocation. In short, my life seemed to offer only the prospect of an empty and lonely desert, which gave me little sense of meaning or identity. And all of this I was to pray for as the highest spiritual poverty? This was not the highest; it was the worst.

Only gradually did grace begin to open me to the possibility that my only real meaning and identity were to be found in Christ. I learned that the desert-like emptiness of my life (as I was anticipating it) would be the place where I discovered the Lord in a way that had never been possible before. Work, success, projects, satisfying and intense relationships (in general an extraordinarily rich life) had all contributed to still, if not to fully silence, the deepest yearnings of my being. Only in the feared desert did I learn that the dreaded "worst" was a gift and source of gratitude: the discovery that, in spite of surface protests to the contrary, I really did love God overwhelmingly more than any job, or living in any particular place. I could well say with St. Augustine, "Late have I loved you, O Beauty ever ancient, ever new, late have I loved you!"[1]

The Exercise on the two standards not only stretched my openness towards a future which was in God's hands and not mine. It also enlightened me about my past as well. For when I looked at the standard of Christ (poverty, contempt, humility), I also had to consider the opposing standard (riches, honor, and pride) as it had occasion to function in my life. Specifically, I thought about the work I had been doing. It was exactly what I loved to do. It satisfied and nourished me (riches). Moreover, I did it very well and competently, so people appreciated it (honor). Finally, I had begun to think in terms of *my* work and *my* skills (pride), rather than God's work and God's gifts.

Recognizing the way of the enemy (riches, honor, pride) was one matter. Turning towards the way of Christ (poverty, contempt, humility) was quite another. David Fleming's *Contemporary Reading of the Spiritual Exercises* was of some help here. Fleming writes:

> . . . if I have nothing, my only possession is Christ and this is to be really true to myself—the humility of a person whose whole reality lies in being created and redeemed in Christ.[2]

I could not say that I did not want Christ to be my sole possession, and yet. . . . The struggle with this Exercise felt like a process of being torn apart. My prayers amounted to a genuine battle with God in which I was doomed to defeat and from which I emerged feeling tattered and exhausted. At one point I even asked Jesus, "Why do you want me to be unhappy?" I truly felt that God's road was leading me into places and choices which would be bleak indeed. In fact, I thought I was being torn away from where I would be able to do ministry, to be an apostle. Hence my anger with Ignatius who sees the highest spiritual poverty associated with apostleship. To me it seemed I was being denied the apostleship and stuck with the poverty—a foul deal to be sure. I sobbed with frustration and perhaps in mourning over some of the old creation which was having trouble passing away.

During this long and painful struggle, I wondered angrily at times whether God wanted me at all. But I was still thinking of myself in terms of what I *do*. I realized with a sudden clarity and a new lightness that God did not need what I might do but wanted in fact just me, and that was precisely what I had been withholding. Too tired for further resistance, I felt peace but also a certain sadness, a feeling I have experienced after giving birth. It took a while to move from the storm of that battle to a quiet and self-forgetting moment. Nor had any amount of resolution or hard work on my part been able to move me beyond my ego-centric anxiety. The unexpected and total gratuitousness of the moment of liberation was clearly beyond my capacities to obtain, desire, or even imagine. To love God is only possible because God does the impossible in us.

Two Faces of God

After the solitary time of preparation in Nazareth, the turning toward the temple at Jerusalem, and the challenge of the "two standards," the *Spiritual Exercises* follow Jesus onto the road of service and mission. The next two contemplations form an initiation into this ministry and show two different faces of the God before whom he and we stand.

Jesus, having set out from home, was baptized by John in the Jordan River, saw the Spirit in the form of a dove, and heard the voice of God: "This is my beloved Son, with whom I am well pleased" (Matt. 3:17). That Mary, Jesus, and the Father should again be companions on this journey seemed very natural to me. I could imagine the sadness and confusion of Mary when Jesus left home, uncertain himself about the future paths of his life. I wondered if she felt useless now, or questioned the meaning of her own existence. Did she see bleak emptiness in the days stretching before her?

My time of prayer spent with Mary was quiet and reflective, as was the time I then spent with Jesus as he began his travels. Arriving at the Jordan, I recognized it as that place which I had so often visited in my imagination when I desperately needed to find solace—a stream of clear water, radiant in the sun and flowing over a beautiful rocky riverbed. We stood together with many others in this living stream, and I saw with astonishment the simplicity and humility of Jesus who accepted this baptism of repentance along with all the rest of us. It was a moment of knowing that the God of Jesus Christ had really accepted the ambiguity of our human life.

For a while I simply stood and watched the scene and knew that I wanted not merely to watch but also to participate, to be one with all the others and one with Christ—which seemed, in fact, to me the same thing. I asked Jesus to baptize me also, and he poured the water over my head.

After the baptism, as St. Luke records, Jesus remained at prayer, experienced the presence of the Holy Spirit to him, and heard the Father call him "Beloved" (Luke 3:21-22). At the same time, while doing this Exercise, I felt as if God also spoke such words to me: "You are my beloved daughter. My favor rests on you." I was overwhelmed and also frightened now. By what blasphemous arrogance dare I hear such a thing? Surely my imagination had gone too far this time!

Then I remembered the others to whom God had spoken the words "beloved child." Mary had heard herself called, in the words of an angel, "highly favored one." The Annunciation was not simply the offering and acceptance of a mysterious fate and a heavy burden. It was a gentle invitation to a most loving intimacy between the human and the divine. In her *Dialogue*, Catherine of Siena always hears herself addressed by God as "beloved daughter." In the *Imitation of Christ*, Thomas a Kempis sees himself as a "dear son" to the Lord. And in the 1980s, a young friend of mine in Massachusetts had drawn a pencil line through "dear son" wherever it occurs in that book, and had written between the lines "dear daughter." She too was able to hear herself addressed in familial terms by the God of creation. I saw with delight that, because of such humble things as the baptism of Jesus by John, it had now become possible for human ears to hear a God who calls them "beloved" and "children," and who takes pleasure in them.

It was in the joyful aftermath of the baptism, when Jesus had experienced the empowering intimacy of the Father's love and the indwelling presence of the Holy Spirit, that his journey brought him to that place where God is felt to be absent—the desert. I saw now that the Spirit—and not the devil—led him into the wilderness where he was alone, hungry, and tempted. Since the Spirit was leading, I continued my companionship with Jesus on his way even here.

There was, at first, a light and humorous quality to this desert. I imagined myself and Jesus (looking like a couple of rustic hermits) sitting on straw mats on the sand in front of a little hut. It was a unique and exciting opportunity. All alone in this wasteland, I felt no distractions and was free to say whatever came to mind. For a while I poured out my problems, needs, desires. And Jesus listened to the torrent of words, very patiently. He just sat on his mat and listened. All he said was, "I want you to stay with me in this desert." I was very willing indeed.

No one and nothing could interfere with this time alone with Jesus. So I thought. But I had not reckoned with the presence of the temptor. Nor did I understand the silence of God in our deserts. After a while, I stopped my monologue and realized that perhaps we were not sitting here so that I could have answers to all my questions. I was to become quiet and simply stay where I was—on my straw mat. To experience what Ignatius called the "application of the senses" with regard to the desert can sometimes mean a true poverty of spirit. God may be saying, "I have fed you with milk and honey, but now you will have plain food or no food that you can recognize at all. Can you love me for my own sake?" To be quiet, patiently listening and waiting can sometimes seem like fasting. It is hard not to run from the loneliness of such solitude and silence. It is very hard to be patient.

The desert where I watched and listened had now become a much more austere and frightening place than it had seemed at first. Jesus was sitting back on his heels praying, his hands covering his face. The sun was blazing overhead and a howling wind blew dust and sand at us. We were each wearing a rough brown blanket or cloak to protect ourselves from the blowing sand. I simply sat and watched the prayer of Jesus. From time to time, he lifted up his face and I could see tears squeezed from between closed eyelids. I saw that he was in great anguish—and fear. The intensity of his struggle overwhelmed me. Powerless, I knelt in the sand, my cloak covering my head and face, and said over and over, "My Lord."

The time of temptation seemed very long, as I huddled near the ground in the shelter of my cloak. Eventually, however, the sun was lower in the sky. Soon we needed our cloaks for protection against the evening cold. The Jesus I watched was weak, exhausted, fragile—very human. The realization of his humanness filled me with awe. Was it because of this that "God highly exalted him" (Phil. 2:9)?

When the time of temptation had finally passed, I looked upon the face of Jesus. It was haggard and dusty. But he lifted it to the sky which was clear, ablaze with stars, and very beautiful. The wind had ceased its howling. As the stars shone upon the face of the one I now knew I loved, it became again peaceful and luminous. Jesus looked up into the light and spoke the word "Father." The communicating love of the Spirit was in some way visible in that gaze of one, radiant in the starry night, who looked towards God. And I, sitting wrapped in a blanket on the desert floor, knew myself to be sister, daughter, and beloved. I was surrounded by and penetrated with that Trinity I had come to know in the living waters and in the anguish of the desert.

Come and See

At the beginning of the ministry of Jesus, after his baptism and temptation, Ignatius has us consider the call of the various disciples. In this way the Exercises link the mission of Jesus directly and immediately to the vocation of the Christian. The Lord does not go about the work of establishing the Kingdom and then appoint followers to keep it running smoothly.

Rather, from the very beginning of the public ministry, the building of the Kingdom is a reality which becomes visible and is known in the existence of a community of believers who stand in the presence of Jesus and participate in his life.

It is striking to read John's account of the first two disciples who leave John the Baptist for the company of Jesus (John 1:35-39). Andrew and his companion do not ask what they should do, nor even what it is that Jesus does. Rather they ask him, "Where do you stay?" Jesus replies, "Come and see." Belonging to him implies, first of all, being in his presence. Finding, seeing, and knowing Jesus are keys to discipleship. So too the prophetic mission of John the Baptist is most eloquent in his simple pointing away from himself to this other who is to come after him.

The disciple who does great work, but does not point beyond his or her own individuality to the beckoning Jesus, becomes in him- or herself an object of the seeker's pursuit, instead of the Lord. The seeker has no opportunity to ask, "Rabbi, where do you live?" And there is no space in which the words of Jesus may be heard: "Come and see." When I read the stories of the call of the disciples, I remembered the people in my own life who had pointed out Jesus, who had been quiet enough in their own ministry that I could hear the words, "Come and see." Those people were the translucent ones—the windows which enabled me to see through their clarity into the house of the Lord. Through them I was able to ask the question, "Where do you stay?"

It occurred to me then that the discipleship of those faithful followers had not so much to do with the greatness of their deeds (although some did accomplish much good) nor with the absence of sin from their lives. Clearly that was not the case. The original disciples lost faith, were fickle and timid, quarreled over their rank in the Kingdom. The contemporaries who had pointed out Jesus to me were just as prone to fall from grace as they were—or I was.

At this point, I found myself confronted with a troubling

mystery. I passionately desired that my whole life should point towards Jesus, should be a transparent window for his light. And yet it was clear that I was by no means free from temptation and sin. How could this be? I was perplexed. How could I (or anyone) love God and still sin?

In distress and confusion, I asked Jesus, "How can you be with me and this still happen?" Still attentive to John's account of the call of the first disciples, I read the words of John the Baptist: "Look! There is the Lamb of God who takes away the sin of the world!" (John 1:29). With astonishment, as if I had never really heard those words before, I said to Jesus, "I thought you were the one who takes away the sin of the world." But I was thinking, "Then why don't you?" And very gently the answer came: "I do, whenever you turn to me." I realized that that was true—again and again.

As had often happened before, the answer that was given did not exactly correspond to the question asked. But I knew also that the answer was a true one. I had simply asked the wrong question. I had become so preoccupied with my apparent dilemma that I forgot to "come and see."

The call to "come and see" is no guarantee of perfection. It is not spoken to the perfect at all. In reading of the call of Matthew (Matt. 9:9-13), the Pharisee in me had to notice the pleasure Jesus seemed to take in the company of sinners. It was I to whom the words were spoken:

> Go and learn the meaning of the words, "I desire mercy, not sacrifice." I did not come to call the righteous but sinners.
> (Matt. 9:13)

The knowledge that this was so, that Jesus will sit at table and eat, and build the Kingdom of God with sinners—like the tax collector Matthew, and the first disciples, and me—filled me with gladness and thanksgiving.

I had wondered how one can be in the company of Jesus and still sin. Turning to Luke's account of the call of Peter (after a miraculous catch of fish), I was surprised to read that Peter fell to his knees and said, "Depart from me, Lord, for I am a sinful man" (Luke 5:8). At last I had come to see. I could only say, "Do not leave me, Lord. I am a sinful person."

Abundant Life

I had never understood why the miracle at Cana was all so important. We were house-hunting when I did this Exercise, and I was painfully ambivalent. Was it possible to be a Christian and own real estate? I had been formed during the '60s to believe in the value of only those things which advanced social justice, human rights, and world peace. And yet the children needed a stable home, preferably with swings in the back yard. My own feeling was that, without a sunny spot for a garden, I should be perpetually unhappy. While driving to appointments with various real estate agents, I contemplated the wedding feast at Cana.

It occurred to me then that the Cana story was at once simple and gracious. Mary's comment is very straightforward: "They have no wine" (John 2:3). Her expectation reflects an unequivocal trust that Jesus will handle the situation helpfully. As indeed he does. Now it was clear to me that water would have been sufficient to quench thirst, and inexpensive wine quite adequate for a celebration among well-wishers. The act of Jesus exceeds necessity, however, in that he graciously provides not merely the bare essentials, but something of richness and beauty—something which gives pleasure. It is the only miracle we have recorded in which Jesus provides solely for the enjoyment of friends. All the rest (healings, exorcisms, calming a storm, raising the dead) are compassionate responses to human suffering and need, and bring about a restoration of health, holiness, and faith. This miracle is different, purely gratuitous. The wine is a noble one, better than the finest from the host's own cellars:

> Everyone serves good wine first, and then when people have drunk freely, an inferior one; but you have kept the good wine until now.
> (John 2:10)

Moved by this sign of divine extravagance, I said, in words like Mary's: "Lord, we have no home," and felt strangely confident that we would have one, not just grim adequacy, but a place where there would be the possibility of growth, beauty, and play. As it happened, the house we found was very small, but there were swings and a sunny place to grow a garden. I have always thought of that house as the place of the wedding feast at Cana. It became for me a sign of gratuitous generosity and a place for celebrating the feast of life. It also made me know that God calls us also to deal with one another with the same lavish prodigality. To have received everything from the hand of God, to suffer neither guilt in accepting it nor greed in demanding more, gives us the freedom and the ministry of being sacraments of the same overflowing love and abundance for others.

The image of the feast now seemed to predominate in the way I saw God's dealings with human beings. Continuing the same Exercise on the wedding feast of Cana, I prayed, "Jesus, please lead me into your wedding feast." And for a moment it seemed that he did. The feast was very beautiful—an instant of happiness which left me feeling totally content, although I cannot say at all in what that beauty, happiness, and contentment consisted. My prayers during this time remained difficult to describe. In fact, I might say that I was not praying then at all. In some way my will to have autonomy and remain in control had yielded and was no longer waging war against God as it had done in the past. It had simply stepped aside. This was a time of peace when I knew, with St. Paul, the praying of the Spirit within me (Rom. 8:15-16, 26).

The divine feast, which most often I had not even noticed or only occasionally glimpsed dimly, now became "visible" to me as the fabric of our corporate life. It was a communion in which I saw two things most clearly: that we are fed by God's own hand, and that that nourishment is the life which binds us together in a most intimate connection, transcending any borders of time and space.

Once I had the unusual leisure to spend an hour alone in a church with a very simple chapel of the Blessed Sacrament. I sat in this chapel, on a chair not three feet from a lovely old tabernacle. My thoughts were very scattered at first. After a while many people became present to my mind: friends, family, co-workers, figures from my past of whom I had not thought in years—former teachers, former students. It seemed that all of these were now also present in the small chapel.

Being by now very familiar with the procedures of Ignatius, I first sought the companionship and intercession of Mary—and felt indeed that she was standing right next to me. I must have felt in need of extra support, because I next turned also to Ignatius himself. And he was there as well, standing on the other side of me. I was singing the Litany of the Saints to myself, freely inserting names as they occurred to me. Nor did I restrict myself to names of the canonized, but gladly added the martyrs of our own time to the list: Jean Donovan, Ita Ford, Maura Clarke, Dorothy Kazel, Oscar Romero. The presence of the saints was a strength and support to me.

My thoughts, which had been so scattered, were now still. There was nothing at all for me to say, think, or do. I was completely silent, and just sat looking at the gilded wooden tabernacle, so close to me and at eye level. And then it was as if Christ were standing right beside it, palpably present before me, as alive and as genuinely there in the room as any human being might have been—more so. He brought in his hands the communion I so desired.

At the moment of receiving the Bread, all the world was included: whole countries and peoples, as well as all the friends I had been thinking about. We were one in this Body of Christ, connected, not separate at all. Then with the cup of wine, I was asked a question: "Do you truly want my life to be your own?" I barely breathed the answer: "Yes, Lord, I truly want your life to be my life." Deeply changed by an unfathomable grace, I felt that this was true. I was anchored, rooted in Christ and knew, as I sat there, the presence of the Trinity in and around me. On the antique tabernacle, a pelican fed her young and a dove hovered overhead. From outside the church, I heard the sound of birds, traffic, and noisy children.

The King

Ignatius allows in his notes that the second week may be lengthened or shortened in a way appropriate to the progress of the individual retreat [162]. The purpose of the contemplations on the life of Christ is to bring a person into intimate contact with that life, so that the choices he or she makes will be increasingly conformed to that life. Throughout the week, the grace we are seeking is a deep knowledge and love of Jesus which will bring us also to follow him more closely. It is the intersection of the life recorded in the Gospels with our own lived history which is the dynamic principle of the *Spiritual Exercises*.

Arriving in the course of the second week at the contemplation of the Sermon on the Mount, I discovered that I had now returned to the point from which I had begun. Here again was the proclamation of a new creation. Jesus sets forth, with the Beatitudes, a blueprint for the Kingdom. The second week ends with the triumphal entry into Jerusalem on Palm Sunday. The King is acclaimed as he enters the city where he will face a cruel and lonely death. It is a return to the Exercise on the Kingdom with which Ignatius begins this second week.

The person I want to follow stands on a grassy hillside and speaks such paradoxical words: "Blessed are the poor in spirit, for theirs is the kingdom of heaven" (Matt. 5:3). The Lord I want to serve walks amid a rejoicing crowd, surrounded by friends and well-wishers who carry flowers and palm branches: "Blessed is he who comes in the name of the Lord!" (Matt. 21:9). The Savior stands before another crowd: "Crucify him!" (Luke 23:21). The King is enthroned, but only a few remain: ". . .today you will be with me in Paradise" (Luke 23:43).

Notes

[1]*Confessions*, X, 27, trans. R. S. Pine-Coffin, (New York: Penguin, 1961), 231.
[2]P. 89.

Chapter Five
Compassion and Grief: The "Third Week"

The Colloquy as Being There

Because of the intimacy involved during the contemplations of the Passion, it might be well to review some aspects of the time called "colloquy." Just as in human situations of taking care of the sick or of ministering to the dying our presence is often more important than our faltering words or awkward actions, so too *to be with* Christ in his Passion describes our prayer response at this time better than any words or actions. Previously we described the colloquy as the intimate conversation between friends. Now we open out that description to include the depth of feeling, love, and compassion, which allows us just *to be there*.[1]

Fleming's words on the contemplation of the Passion bring us to the heart of the matter of the "third week" of the *Spiritual Exercises*. Being there is the hardest thing. When someone—someone we love—is suffering, we want to make it better, to fix everything, to stop the pain or anesthetize the sufferer. Barring those possibilities, we become angry, resentful, frustrated, or depressed. We turn away; we run away. If forced to remain, we avert our eyes, look to other corners of the room or the universe, to events of the past or our hopes for the future. If all else fails we fall asleep. Fleming continues in the note quoted above:

> We should remember that faced with the suffering of the Passion we may have to pray even for the gift of letting ourselves want to experience it with Christ.[2]

My father was dying. He had been rushed to the hospital with a complicated case of pneumonia and respiratory failure. After the brief airplane flight, during which I tried not to think about any of it, my initial visit to the Intensive Care Unit made my knees buckle. This was frightening. Someone who had always been in control of things was suddenly, inexplicably, no longer in control and very vulnerable. He could not make himself understood very well because of the oxygen mask over his mouth and nose. Repeatedly he said he felt "rotten." His breathing was labored and erratic. He could not keep his hands from shaking. He said he was not in pain, but agitation and anxiety were to be seen in his eyes. I watched and listened.

After the first day in the hospital my father was placed on a respirator because he was "too tired to breathe." Ever articulate, he was now wholly unable to speak. We tried to guess his questions and requests. He formed letters and words on a pad of paper, but his hand trembled too violently. No one could read the markings which resembled a series of lightning bolts.

Being present in that place was a difficult thing. The family visits to the ICU were limited to fifteen minutes every three hours. Between those visits we sat in a small waiting room and found ourselves falling asleep—from weariness or fear? Both Mark and Matthew record that Jesus upbraids the disciples for sleeping during his anguished hours of prayer in Gethsemane:

> Could you not keep watch for one hour? Watch and pray that you may not undergo the test. The spirit is willing but the flesh is weak (Mark 14:37-38; cf. Matt. 26:40-41).

But the Gospel of Luke takes a somewhat more generous attitude towards this sleep: "When he rose from prayer and returned to his disciples, he found them sleeping from grief" (Luke 22:45). Sitting together in the waiting room outside of the ICU, we slept from time to time. Who can say if we were fleeing from the consciousness of our fear and our father's suffering, or simply exhausted from the weight of that very consciousness?

My father himself seemed fearful as to the outcome of this illness. When he could communicate by gesture or writing, he seemed most concerned with knowing the date and the time, then with his medical condition and prognosis. Once he asked if he were going to die. We did not know what to answer. Our ability to think and reflect seemed to be malfunctioning. I was only able to register the present tense. When anyone said something about the past or the future it struck me as being absurdly irrelevant. What mattered was *now*, being there in the present moment, being there and being conscious.

Flying back home, I bore with me vivid images of my stricken father. Jesus in the garden had prayed, begged for release from his anguish, had wept and sweated blood when the shadow of death passed over the horizon of his consciousness. These images began to coalesce with the memory of my father's face behind the oxygen mask. Suddenly frightened, I wanted to run away from the intersection of those two agonies. I was afraid to see what I was really seeing, what had been visible to me from time to time during the past weekend. The fear of death—Jesus' and my father's—was of an intensity which terrified me. I prayed that I might not fall asleep. The watching and listening, the fear and incapacity, the long process of dying were to last for the next nine months. Those who were most present, my mother and my brother, would desire more than once to run away. Even at a distance, I fell asleep—sometimes from fear and sometimes from the weariness that accompanies watching that which we cannot bear to look upon.

"The Killing Fields"

Sometimes "being there" in the presence of the suffering Christ can take surprising forms. The 1985 movie, *The Killing Fields*, was one such surprise. It is a story of one person's exodus from a land of bloodshed and fear to freedom and eventual reunion with his family.

Dith Pran, a Cambodian photographer working for the *New York Times* waited too long to be evacuated from his ravaged country. Out of loyalty to his American colleague, Sidney Schanberg, Pran delays his escape until it is in fact no longer possible for Cambodian nationals to leave the country. There is an awful scene when he is obliged to leave the safety of the French embassy where he has taken refuge with a number of foreign journalists. One watches with fear and horror as Pran goes back through the gates of the embassy. He must flee as best he can before the cultural purge of the Khmer Rouge, who devastate the countryside, destroying all traces of intellectual life and technology—from books to automobiles—and kill the educated whom they see as culturally contaminated. Pran journeys on foot through episodes of danger and real horror on his way to freedom which he finds at a refugee camp inside the border of Thailand. He has suffered cruelty and violence, hunger, and exhaustion along the way.

After seeing this film for the first time, I returned the very next night to see it again. The plot was vivid in my memory. What I had returned for were the sounds and the images. I wanted to absorb within my being, to engrave indelibly upon myself, the scenes of pain and cruelty, but also the scenes of beauty and kindness which were in that film. I had a sense that in this movie there was truth. It later occurred to me that what I was doing by this double exposure to *The Killing Fields* was a modern form of the Ignatian "repetition," a way of entering more deeply into a text by repeating my contemplation of it. This particular repetition might, in fact, be seen as an "application of the senses," because in this second viewing I was able to detach my attention from the actual events in the passover of Dith Pran, in order to *see* and to *listen* more acutely. I sunk myself as deeply as possible into the sensory experience of war and destruction recorded by the film.

In my "application of the senses" of *The Killing Fields*, three scenes were particularly vivid. At one point Pran has been brutally beaten by his captors. He is kneeling on the ground with his arms bound behind him. His face and body are disfigured with blood and dirt. It is John's Gospel which provides the text to accompany this vision:

> Then Pilate took Jesus and had him scourged. And the soldiers wove a crown out of thorns and placed it on his head, and clothed him in a purple cloak. . . . So Jesus came out, wearing the crown of thorns and the purple cloak. And he said to them, "Behold, the man!" (John 19:1-2, 5).

I looked at the man, although it was difficult not to look away. He suffered in innocence, and it was amazing to me that the harvest of such violence was gentleness and love. Throughout his ordeal, Pran remains a person of quiet compassion, neither hardened and insensitive nor returning the hatred he experiences.

The second scene which impressed itself most vividly upon my soul during my "repetition" of The Killing Fields takes place in a hospital in Phnom Penh after an American bombing of the city. Wounded victims, civilian residents of the capital, are lying everywhere waiting for medical care. Blood is literally flowing over the floor and down the stairs—the blood of the suffering innocent.

The third scene takes place during Pran's long journey. He is walking along a narrow slip of land by the muddy waters of a flooding river. Here the bodies of many of those killed have been washed up. Pran comes unprepared upon the grisly scene. He falls suddenly into a pit filled with skeletons and partially decayed corpses. The shock and horror of this experience washed through me. In some way I lived that gruesome moment in my own flesh.

After the experience of contemplating The Killing Fields, I was present at a liturgical celebration in my parish church. Although very attentive to the events taking place in the present, I seem to have carried with me the events recorded in the film. I kept seeing the people and land of Cambodia. That moment in twentieth-century history was intensely and really present to me, and became increasingly so as the liturgy continued. I listened to the words of the prayers, responded at the proper times, and sang all the hymns. But I was seeing Cambodia, the killing fields. The priest said, "Lift up your hearts," and tears began to run down my face and did not stop until after Communion. The priest said, "This is the cup of my blood of the new covenant. . ." and I saw again the hospital in Phnom Penh. The blood of children and adults flowed over the floor and down the stairs. I looked at the chalice of the Blood of Christ and saw the blood of the Cambodian people.

Later that day I sat on the porch and watched the patterns of sunlight filtered through leaves. I heard the children playing, other sounds of the neighborhood, and the background drone of traffic. I reflected on the presence of God in the history of Cambodia and in all of human history. I had seen and accepted the identity of Christ with the suffering innocent. But now my complacency was shattered by the realization that not only the victims, but also the perpetrators, the fanatics, the ones who hated or were cruelly indifferent, were also present in that identity. Jesus had always been found among the sinners, eating with them and loving them. Christ was now in the bomber pilots, the leaders who made military decisions, the comfortable voters who elected them, the corrupt petty officials, the ruthless dictators, the American presidents, all of us. To bear the sins of the world meant to bear the violence done in Cambodia. All of it was present in that raised cup of wine. And I too was part of this passion, connected with all of it. The victims, the merciful helpers, the perpetrators, and the indifferent: all were present and at one in that poured out blood.

The Cup of Salvation

It is helpful when beginning the third week of the *Spiritual Exercises* to remember the point of the meditation on the Kingdom which began the second week. There we sought to commit ourselves as fully as possible to a share with Christ in the building of the Kingdom: in the labor, the hardships, the weariness, as well as in the eventual victory. In the contemplations on the passion and death of Jesus, we are plunged into the heart of that commitment. We want to participate as fully as possible in the fate of the Lord, not because we perversely desire to witness or undergo suffering, nor yet because we have some abstract notion about its purifying and strengthening qualities. Our sole desire throughout the Exercises is to be at one with Christ, to be ever more fully his image. This identity only grows to the extent that we come to know him deeply. Such knowledge is only born in our experiential presence to him. It is not the knowing of cognition but of love.

In the third week, the prescribed grace for which we pray during our contemplation of the passion is a difficult one:

> It belongs to the Passion to ask for grief with Christ in grief, anguish with Christ in anguish, tears and interior pain at such great pain which Christ suffered for me. [203]

We should not assume that these times of prayer will be serene and comforting. We are not considering serene and comforting events. There may be then a great deal of inner resistance to our serious confrontation with them. Fleming writes, "...faced with the suffering of the Passion we may have to pray even for the gift of letting ourselves want to experience it with Christ."[3]

When making the Exercises of the third week, I often had to pray for the grace even to want to experience them. Although on a conscious level I felt committed to this process and did in fact desire a closer union with Christ, what went on at other levels amounted at times to mutiny. My body would either refuse to sit still or else it would fall soundly asleep. My mind wandered freely. At times my brain felt like a badly tuned radio which was receiving at least three channels at once.

I was considering the time Jesus spent praying in the garden, his abandonment by friends and disciples, and his arrest. I had forcibly to refocus my attention on the scene. My mind seemed eager to fix on the least distraction which came by. I saw the disciples fleeing and said, "Oh, Peter, where were you all this time?" and heard Jesus saying to me, "Where are you all this time?" Like Peter, I was either asleep in the garden, warming my hands at a safe distance in the courtyard, or gone from the scene totally.

Moved by the question, I reflected for a while on my real desires and said, "Lord, I want to stay with you. I do not want to run away. I do not want to be separated from you." At that moment, as I watched, someone struck Jesus in the face. I recoiled in shock as if I myself had been struck, and again I had to force myself to pay attention. However, my ability to do so grew worse and worse.

What I heard from Jesus was only one protest:

Have you come out as against a robber, with swords and clubs, to seize me? Day after day I was with you teaching in the temple area, yet you did not arrest me (Mark 14:48-49).

I thought of his relationship to the temple throughout his life, how important it had been: his presentation there by his parents, his eagerness as an adolescent to converse with the rabbis and to ask them questions, his reading the Scriptures in the synagogue at Nazareth. His involvement with public worship and religious teaching had been long-standing. Yet here was a priest whose relationship to the structures of his own religion was one of rejection, and whose blood is the sacrifice which gives entrance into the house of God, the temple not built by human hands (see Heb. 10:19).

What I saw was one, in an agony of spirit, lying on the ground. He raised his eyes to see a cup. Holding it in his hands and yet at arm's length, he said, "This is the cup of my blood." He held out the cup towards me: "Drink the cup of my blood." I shrank back. This was a very difficult moment. How could anyone embrace such a priesthood? Here were swords and clubs, but no honor in the temple. After a while, but still hesitating, I reached for that chalice and drank the bitter wine, sipped only a drop, yet still the fragrance and the taste of it penetrated my entire being. Overwhelmed with fear and gladness, I watched. He clutched the cup now closely to his breast. A shudder passed through his body—and words: ". . . yet, not as I will, but as you will" (Matt. 26:39).

Release to the Captive

Vivid before my eyes was the scene instigated by Pilate. The crowd was given a choice: freedom for Jesus or for that insurgent and murderer, Barabbas (Luke 23:13-25). The crowd screamed out the name of Barabbas and demanded that Jesus be crucified. I watched the painful ordeal of the captive. Against the screams of the crowd I quietly spoke the name Jesus over and over, as if in softly speaking that loved name there were some kind of healing counterpoint to the vehemence and hatred which were shrieking all around me.

The one who silently watches the sufferings of the captive is simply present. It is not often possible to grant release to prisoners. Being there with them is a time of dark faith that God will, against all odds and in spite of appearances,

> ...bring glad tidings to the poor,
> ...proclaim liberty to captives
> and recovery of sight to the blind,
> let the oppressed go free... (Luke 4:18).

In an hour of prayer, I saw the prisoner bound and delivered over by Pilate to be tortured. I saw again the beaten body of the Cambodian photographer Dith Pran with arms tied behind his back. He had been left alone and half-conscious. I saw my father bound to the respirator which gave him breath and life for six months but deprived him of all freedom, even the ability to speak. I watched the railroad cars carrying their millions of human victims to the Nazi death camps. I saw Native Americans driven from their homes and dying on forced marches to reservations. Prisoners of war, soldiers and civilians of all ages and countries, I saw led in chains from one place of captivity to another. Again and again throughout all of human history, Israel was being led into yet another exile.

As the captives passed before my eyes in all their helplessness, I was nonetheless aware that God was in some way present to them all, was an integral part of their experience, whether they were conscious of that divine participation or not. I watched Jesus, still bound, but now standing before Herod (Luke 23:8-11). He was silent, and surely discouraged, lonely, and frightened. Clearly he was exhausted. How is it possible that the God of creation is present to this situation, to this man of sorrows? John Shea writes in *Stories of God:*

> ...the Cross is the symbol of the fellow suffering of God.... The love of God demands he be wherever his creation is.
>
> The Cross of Christ is the penetration of God into that unholy area where we would least expect him and, if the truth be known,

where we least want him. God has entered into the loneliness of our suffering and the self-hatred of our sin.[4]

The incarnation was a painful embrace. I read again the letter to the Philippians:

> Have among yourselves the same attitude that is also yours
> in Christ Jesus,
> Who, though he was in the form of God,
> did not regard equality with God something to be grasped.
> Rather, he emptied himself,
> taking the form of a slave,
> coming in human likeness;
> and found human in appearance,
> he humbled himself,
> becoming obedient to death,
> even death on a cross (Phil. 2:6, 8).

The early Christian hymn proclaims what God is like. I looked upon the face of a slave, a prisoner, a weary and comfortless pilgrim, one of the homeless. In that face—in all the faces of the poor, the prisoners, the outcast—was God. In the moment of really seeing, with eyes opened by grace, I worshipped God in fragile human form.

After a while I found myself, along with Jesus, a prisoner in a Roman jail. Some soldiers had severely beaten him and then shoved him into a corner near me. I recognized him, had heard him preach from a boat to a great crowd of followers, had listened to his words on the grassy mountainside. I had loved him from a distance. Now, having bribed the guards for a little water, I brought it over to this Jesus. He drank a little bit. I was acutely aware of his innocence, while I myself was in prison for my crimes. Feeling awkward and ashamed, I poured the rest of the water on his hands and back. He was still bleeding and I saw that now some of his blood was on my hands. In that moment I was transformed and healed.

It was only then that I noticed I was chained. There was a large manacle around one ankle and attached to the floor with a heavy chain. Jesus said to me, "I want you to be free." At once the chains fell away. Deeply weary but at peace, I lay on the floor and fell asleep. Soon, however, the soldiers returned and dragged Jesus away with them. I was free to leave, to escape from this grim place. But I wanted to remain with the one who had let me know my freedom, and even to return it to him as a gift. I wanted to follow Jesus.

Where This Following Leads

Margaret Craven's novel, *I Heard the Owl Call My Name*,[5] can provide a helpful commentary to the contemplations on the Crucifixion. The hero, Mark Brian, a newly ordained Anglican priest, is sent by his bishop to the Indian village of Kingcome in British Columbia. The bishop knows that this young man has contracted an incurable disease and that he will certainly not live longer than three years. This information the bishop does not at first share with the priest whom he sees as not yet ready for death. The assignment to the Indian mission is a way to introduce him to as real an experience of life—unbuffered by cultural habit and convention—as possible. It will not be possible to accept death before he knows what living is. The pastoral assignment will be a difficult exposure to ministry in the midst of an alien cultural environment, in real material poverty, among naturally reticent people. There will be no comfortable supports and distractions to dull or obscure the process of being a human being among other human beings: of learning to know himself and them. The bishop believes that his priest will find at the very heart of life that which will enable him to die.

In his life among the Kwakiutl tribe, Mark Brian experiences loneliness and physical hardship. He shares the suffering of a hunting and fishing people whose way of life is dying. The village is increasingly drained by the flight of its youth to education, technology, and life in the cities. In his two years in Kingcome, the young vicar comes to know death most intimately. Upon his arrival there is the body of a little boy laid out in the vicarage and awaiting burial. He attends at the dying of a woman giving birth to her sixth child, and at the passing of a solitary old logger.

Most significant is his contemplation of the yearly journey of the salmon, "the swimmer," to the place of its birth upstream where it will now spawn and die. Mark comes to the stream with a young girl, Keetah, and a wise old woman, his friend Marta. Keetah weeps over the sad end of the swimmer, but Mark comforts her:

> The whole life of the swimmer is one of courage and adventure. All of it builds to the climax and the end. When the swimmer dies, he has spent himself completely for the end for which he was made, and this is not sadness. It is triumph.[6]

It is then that Marta says to him, "The swimmer is your relative. You belong to the salmon people." Mark does, in fact, spend himself completely in the village. He has come to know himself and also the Indians. He now loves the land and its people who are his family. At the end of the novel, it is the bishop who gives words to the process of growth which Mark has experienced in such a short time:

> ...it has always been easier here, where only the fundamentals count, to learn what every [person] must learn in this world.... Enough of the meaning of life to be ready to die.[7]

Mark's death, when it comes, is not the result of his illness but of an accident. He is killed in his boat while searching for a man who has, in fact, already been rescued. Such a death in itself has the potential to be seen as a meaningless and wasteful loss. So too does the death of Jesus who was, after all, neither subversive nor criminal, but innocent. Meaning comes to such a death through a life where faith has nourished wisdom and love.

Karl Rahner calls death the moment of our greatest freedom. This had always seemed an enigma to me. Is it not rather our moment of greatest limitation? In what way does one who is executed as a common criminal, who dies a painful and humiliating death, exercise freedom? Rahner sees death as the final expression of our fallen state, its darkness "the expression, manifestation and revelation of sin in the world."[8] In accepting the darkness of death, Jesus freely transferred the totality of his created self into the hands of his Father. He exercised his greatest freedom in saying "Yes" to the loving embrace of One whom he *at that particular moment* experienced to be absent and to have abandoned him. This freedom is a complete freedom in that it is an acceptance of complete finitude. In a moment of what seems to be annihilation, to choose God above all else, precisely when that "all else" seems to have complete control and to be all that there is, is to respond, as Ignatius has described in the "Principle and Foundation," with indifference (and thus freedom) with regard to all things save the praise, reverence, and service of God.

Thus I observed Jesus approaching the time of his greatest freedom. To watch the slow walk to the place of death was not easy. As I had done so often during the course of the *Spiritual Exercises*, I asked God to lead me to this place, to break down my resistance, to let me see what I was still so fearful of looking at. There were others walking along this way—other women as well. The time was difficult and I succumbed to many distractions. It was hard not to look away from this dying. But, however feebly and inattentively, I watched. Mostly I saw the face of Jesus, a face on which, along with the pain and the love which were so clearly there, was patience. I was surprised and blessed by the patience. I drank deeply of this patience and was able at last not to run away.

To be present and attentive before the cross of Jesus is an experience of prayer which may yield its graces over some length of time. The truth which becomes visible in that place, about who the Lord is and about who I am, is water from a very deep well. One may return to drink from it again and again. It happened that I was reading the Gospel of Luke. In chapter 6, I stopped at the words: "Love your enemies, do good to those who hate you" (6:27). I thought about that for a while. Did I even have any enemies, real enemies? I did not think so. I could not think of anyone who actually hated me. What did this teaching mean for me?

Almost unbidden, there came then to my memory times and

events in my life when I felt, if not hated, certainly unloved. There were many moments of rejection and hurt which now presented themselves to me. Some were forgotten events from my childhood of which I now became painfully conscious. One by one I was aware of these things. Then I also began to remember times in my life when I had inflicted wounds upon others, not because I considered myself their enemy or hated them, but simply out of an ego-centric insensitivity or out of anger at some real or imagined offense. I was seeing the failures of love in my own life history. I felt a great sadness for them—both for the pain I had suffered and for that which I had inflicted. The memories seemed a heavy burden.

While considering these things, I became aware that Jesus had arrived, bearing his cross, at the place of his death. I added all that I had been remembering to that cross, all the voids where there had been no love. And Jesus was stretched out and nailed upon that cross which carried those memories. I knelt and watched as the great weight was lifted up and the cross was put into place in the ground. It was a moment of unimaginable pain that I watched, but also a moment in which love and forgiveness infinitely outweighed the sin and grief which I had brought to it. Not grasping fully what had happened, but deeply grateful, I returned each day for two weeks to this inner place of prayer. It was a contemplation in which I only gradually came to see what God was calling me to see. There was much to see. Beyond the love and pain in the face of Jesus, I also came to see there compassion and acceptance.

Finally and surprisingly, what was revealed to me there was freedom. I had prayed reluctantly for the grace to share in this time of anguish and pain. I had wanted to know Jesus intimately in his passion. Now I saw beyond the physical suffering a different kind of endurance. There was in his situation an awful helplessness and sense of futility. The words rang out: "Save yourself, why don't you? Come down off that cross if you are God's Son!... He saved others but he cannot save himself!" (Matt. 27:40, 42). Jesus did not come down from the cross. He did not save himself. I saw, in this quiet and patient obedience to the final limitation of human autonomy, grace and a mysterious freedom.

In those two weeks of watching I saw, perhaps for the first time, a crucifixion that was real and very close to me. In spite of earlier resistance, I had come face to face with the suffering Jesus. There is not very much that can be said about such an encounter. I became utterly silent. At first it was as if I had wrapped my arms around this cross, which stood so large and palpable before me, and clung to it—clung to it for my very life. Eventually even that image faded from my mind. My prayer before the cross of the dying Jesus was finally simple and empty, empty of thoughts and even of feeling. And yet this silence and emptiness was sufficient, was in fact full of God. Being there was grace enough.

Waiting at the Tomb

Mary was the one for whom God was always doing the impossible. Elizabeth understood that very well. She said, "Blessed are you who believed that what was spoken to you by the Lord would be fulfilled" (Luke 1:45). Now I had followed Mary's waiting beyond the advent months of the silent God hidden in her womb. Again she stood and waited while God remained silent and hidden. How ironic was the resemblance between the words womb and tomb! What did it mean when the psalmist wrote: "Wait for the Lord with courage; be stout-hearted and wait for the Lord" (Ps. 27:14)?

I did not know, but I thought that Mary must know what it meant to wait for the Lord. I asked her to let me stay with her at the tomb of Jesus. The garden there was very peaceful, the olive trees were green with spring. Night had fallen with a clear and brilliantly starry sky. There were other mourners at this tomb, friends and disciples. The merely curious had already departed. There was, after all, nothing of interest to be seen here. Gradually now the friends also left, turning to their evening rest. Some shook their heads, others still wept.

Last of all Mary left the dark and empty garden. Timidly, I also went along on the walk to her house. We stood there together on a porch and turned our faces to the stars. They seemed the only thing left which gave witness to the life of God. I looked back at Mary to see that tears were streaming down her face. Feeling unworthy to be there, I said, "I am one of those who yelled, 'Crucify him.' " Then I said, "He asked God to forgive us, but we *did* know what we were doing." Then I asked Mary to forgive us. We stood there a long time looking at the stars. My face too was wet with tears. After a while she sang very softly:

> My soul proclaims the greatness of the Lord;
> my spirit rejoices in God my savior,
> For he has looked upon his handmaid's lowliness;
> behold, from now on will all ages call me blessed.
>
> (Luke 1:46-48)

Those words were carried by a faith which had underlain her entire life. First spoken at the home of her kinswoman Elizabeth, how much pain and loss had they accompanied? She had bidden farewell to so many now: Elizabeth and the prophet-child John, her own parents, the husband who had welcomed Mystery into his life, and now this one—this child. Grief flowed in her tears and in the words of faith which she spoke once again: "The Mighty One has done great things for me, and holy is his name" (Luke 1:49).

At the end of a long time someone came from inside the house—a young man. Was this the disciple whom Jesus had loved? He brought to the still weeping Mary a cup of warm tea. She sipped it slowly, her whole being an image of sorrow and peace. All three of us stood in silence and looked at the stars. There was comfort here, and promise.

My father, who had always loved snow, died late in January, but there had been no snow that winter. As we left the church and began the slow drive to the cemetery, wet snow began to fall and collect along the sides of the road. When the brief prayer service was over, I stood for a moment and watched. There was the glowing wood of an oak casket covered and surrounded with an extravagance of spring flowers. And the first of the winter's snows fell and melted and ran in droplets down the warmth of waxed wood. Here, too, there was comfort and promise.

Notes

[1]Fleming, p. 119.
[2]Fleming, pp. 119, 121.
[3]Fleming, p. 121.
[4]*Stories of God: An Unauthorized Biography*, (Chicago: Thomas More Press, 1978), p. 151.
[5](Garden City, NY: Doubleday, 1973).
[6]Craven, p. 50.
[7]Craven, pp. 149-150.
[8]*On the Theology of Death*, (New York: Herder and Herder, 1961), p. 61.

Chapter Six
Resurrection: The "Fourth Week"

The Paschal Mystery

To put words to the experience of meeting the risen Lord has never been easy for Christians. While we can—with great variety and vivid detail—describe the history of human sin, the struggles in our individual lives between sin and grace, and while we can movingly retell the stories of the birth, childhood, teaching, public ministry, and suffering and death of Jesus, the Resurrection is another matter entirely. It is a moment of God's transcendent life breaking into our finite world, a time when we can perceive—see, hear, and touch—the reality of eternal life which, for the most part, we only grasp in the dark submission of faith. In the encounter with Jesus—risen, glorified, exalted—our mortal flesh is aware of its intimacy with the infinite holiness and ungraspable enormity of God. Such intimacy is an unthinkable thought, an unspeakable reality, ineffable mystery.

And yet we struggle to wrap words around the mystery. One early Christian tried with powerful poetry to record the actual emergence of the risen Christ from his entombment. In what is now referred to as the apocryphal Gospel of Peter we read:

Now in the night in which the Lord's day dawned, when the soldiers were keeping guard, two by two in every watch, there rang out a loud voice in heaven. They saw the heavens opened, and two men came down from there in great brightness and drew near to the sepulchre. That stone which had been laid against the entrance to the sepulchre started to roll of itself and gave way to the side, and the sepulchre was opened, and both the young men entered in. When then these soldiers saw this, they woke up the centurion and the elders—for they also were there to assist at the watch. And while they were relating what they had seen, they again saw three men come out of the sepulchre, and two of them sustaining the other, and a cross following them. They saw the heads of the two reaching to heaven, but that of him who was led by them by the hand surpassing the heavens. Then they heard a voice crying out of the heavens, "Hast thou preached to them that sleep?" And from the cross there was heard the answer, "Yes."[1]

One should not be surprised that this text never was included in the Christian Church's canon of Scripture. Unlike the more sober and understated canonical Gospels which restricted themselves in their literary rendering of the Resurrection to accounts of finding the empty tomb and of appearances of Jesus after the Resurrection, the Gospel of Peter attempts an imaginary and poetic expression of the inexpressible. The Resurrection is a divine, not a human, event and cannot be encompassed in human words. The Gospel of Peter is, nonetheless, one example of early Christian visionary piety. Like Ignatian contemplation, it reflects the application of the imagination to the saving acts of God in our history. While not accepted as general revelation, such a text may well represent the fruit of contemplative prayer and, like the writings of the great mystics, be the source of inspiration for others.

In the *Spiritual Exercises*, Ignatius asks us to enter with the imaginative vision and insight of faith into the resurrection of Jesus, to take our place within a long history of Christian reflection on and contemplation of the wonder of God's great act in and for Jesus. He asks that we focus our thoughts and imaginations on the divinity of Christ shining through his humanity when he appeared to the disciples after his resurrection. In particular, the grace to be sought during the contemplations of the fourth week is to share in the joy and gladness of the risen Jesus. We seek to know more deeply a Lord in whose presence we find consolation and joy. We pray for the grace to experience Jesus—present to his mother, his disciples, and us—as comforter. The prayer of the fourth week is a contemplation of mystery, the mystery of Christ brought from death to life and appearing to those who love him. In this prayer we may meet the risen Christ, not bound by the limits of time and space, appearing at the moments of sorrow and death in our lives and bringing us the joy of his abundant life.

If I think about the Paschal Mystery itself, Christ's passage through suffering and death to glorious life, I can say very little about it. But there is a simplicity about the *experience* of the Paschal Mystery in my own life about which I can say something. The passage which each Christian undergoes with Christ is symbolically presented in baptism. In the Letter to the Romans, St. Paul writes:

> ...are you unaware that we who were baptized into Christ Jesus were baptized into his death? We were indeed buried with him through baptism into death, so that, just as Christ was raised from the dead by the glory of the Father, we too might live in newness of life.
>
> For if we have grown into union with him through a death like his, we shall also be united with him in the resurrection (Rom. 6:3-5).

The person praying the *Spiritual Exercises* follows the course of Paul's theology of baptism. Having renounced sin (died to it, in Pauline terms), one follows Jesus through the events of his life, contemplates his redemptive suffering and death, and waits with those faithful ones grieving at the tomb. Now in the fourth week, the Christian who has risen from the waters of the tomb of baptism, prays for the grace of joy in the risen Lord.

At the point where the events of our lives intersect with the great story of God's action through Jesus, there we encounter the Paschal Mystery: life, sorrow, suffering, death, and—in shimmering moments—resurrection. To describe such moments is to tell an often surprisingly simple story, even though they are, in fact, glimpses into Mystery.

When the family moved, changed jobs, bade farewell to friends and colleagues, we all died a little bit. We mourned. Three months after the move to a new home, I could still sense the loss within me. I had become aware of an imprecise sadness—a combination of loneliness, isolation, confusion, uncertainty, and a yearning for what had been left behind. These were ordinary feelings, probably recognizable to most people in such circumstances. I wept easily if I saw a sad movie, read a novel, drove my car on a rainy day. I read what St. Paul wrote in the Letter to the Philippians:

> Rejoice in the Lord always. I shall say it again: rejoice! Your kindness should be known to all. The Lord is near. Have no anxiety at all, but in everything, by prayer and petition, with thanksgiving, make your requests known to God. Then the peace of God that surpasses all understanding will guard your hearts and minds in Christ Jesus (Phil. 4:4-7).

Rejoice always! But again I wept. The more I read the rejoicing words, the greater my flow of tears. I could no longer read, but only sobbed. Out of this deep grief which I had finally now expressed without reserve, for the briefest, almost imperceptible moment, I had the impression that the living Jesus was really, palpably there—at my side, comforting me. That was the grace for which, at the behest of Ignatius, I had prayed. The weight of sadness had been washed away in that flood of tears. I felt deeply at peace.

It is only on the other side of grief, when the deaths one suffers have been mourned, that the resurrection can be glimpsed. Loss is an experience which leaves an inner emptiness. But the one who waits at the empty tomb knows that the emptiness is, in fact, pregnant—preparing for the bursting forth of new life. For me, something small and fragile had been fertilized in the empty spaces watered by tears. The growth which began was subtle and hidden, a delicate life, not easy to perceive.

In the stories the evangelists tell of the first Christians' experience of the risen Jesus, something similar happened. They did not see him for who he is. They failed to recognize him. They had been expecting something altogether different. Mary Magdalene, it seems, loved Jesus more than most. I watched her in the garden near his tomb. It was a mild and very quiet spring morning, shortly after sunrise. Mary did not notice the beauty of the sky or of the semi-wild growth of plants surrounding the grassy place. She barely heard the sounds of the first creatures awakening to the day. Her eyes were downcast and, in any event, tears had blurred her vision. Her sandaled feet were brushed by still dewy grass along the path leading to the open tomb. The stone was cool and she leaned against it for a moment before stooping to enter the silent darkness.

Numbness clouded her mind so that even the loveliness and brilliance of the two visitors who were suddenly present could not dislodge the weight of sadness she carried. "Woman, why are you weeping?" Did they really not know why? With leaden steps she turned back to the sunny garden. Her soul had no more seen the heavenly beings than the morning beauty of this place.

There was, however, one whom Mary did notice—a gardener, probably. Here, perhaps, she thought she might find her way to the lost one. She approached him, a smiling, simple figure in a broad-brimmed hat. He seemed a part of the natural setting which she now began to notice a little. The sun moved higher in the sky and the washed garden was bathed in light. Again the words: "Woman, why are you weeping?" Now, mysteriously, there was less of desperate finality in her heart and voice. "Sir, if you carried him away, tell me where you laid him, and I will take him" (John 20:15).

Now it is the face of Jesus that I watch, as he gazes upon the tearful Mary and as he looks into my eyes as well. So much love. A gently bemused smile plays over his features, a smile for the notion that this impulsive follower has just offered to carry off a body heavy with death. I am transfixed by the realization that there are tears in his eyes as well, the tears of gratitude and affection of one who sees himself so loved and mourned.

In the trembling air between them one word hovers, sparkles, and evaporates the clouds before her vision. "Mary." At last she sees. The sun enkindles the garden with vibrating brilliance. "Teacher!" She falls at his feet, reaches for his hand, holds it in her own. But it is not given for us to grasp and possess this moment. "Stop holding onto me." The words are kind. They reveal the depth of his knowledge of her—of me, as well. Such knowledge is also called love.

The vision passes, but the beauty of the morning remains. All is as before but Mary and I can see it now—the flowers, the cool stone, the grassy walk. Where sadness and confusion had been, there now rest an unspeakable peace, a silence, a wonder previously unknown. Mary quickens her steps as she leaves the garden to fulfill her mission, her voice echoing through centuries: "I have seen the Lord!" And I? I too must leave this quiet place. Where there was emptiness, a voice has been born. I have seen the Lord!

The Road to Emmaus

Mary's words are seeds of faith and she has the honor of being the first to carry the good news of the Resurrection. St. Paul writes of such souls in a beautiful passage of the Letter to the Romans:

> But how can they call on him in whom they have not believed? And how can they believe in him of whom they have not heard? And how can they hear without someone to preach? And how can people preach unless they are sent? As it is written, "How beautiful are the feet of those who bring the good news!" ...Thus faith comes from what is heard, and what is heard comes through the word of Christ (Rom. 10:14-15, 17).

But Mary's are not the only feet, nor hers the only voice which makes itself heard. The image in my prayer is no longer the fresh morning garden, but a dusty road. Two travelers hurry along, for the sun is already dropping low in the sky. Their feet involuntarily slow down from time to time. Their hearts are heavy and they speak together quietly. They speak of death—the death of one whom they loved and revered, and the death of hope.

We walk along together (for I have now joined the two as they increase their distance from Jerusalem) and there comes another traveler into our midst. We are not aware of his approach until he has already fallen into step with us. "What are you discussing as you walk along?" What indeed? Their downcast looks and the words which now tumble forth reveal a profound disappointment:

> ...a prophet mighty in deed and word before God and all the people...we were hoping that he would be the one...it is now the third day.... Some women from our group...were at the tomb early in the morning...they had indeed seen a vision of angels ...but him they did not see (Luke 24:19-24).

Then how his gentle laughter caresses their gloominess! The expressive eyes sparkle with affection: "Oh, how foolish you are!" And he teaches us. It is as if a lock upon our minds has been suddenly broken. We hear the Scriptures, the words of Moses and Isaiah resonating in our hearts. It is as if we have never once heard them before this moment. Yes, why did we ever think it could be otherwise? How could we expect a military coup and not even notice that God was there in the suffering of love?

We have come a long way on the road with our talking and now the sun is half set. The evening grows cool and we feel again our forgotten hunger and weariness. We entreat the stranger: "Stay with us, for it is nearly evening and the day is almost over." How many evenings since then have I uttered that prayer! Seated at table, he breaks the bread and shares it with us as if he were the host, we the guests. And I think each one now realizes that that is, in fact, the case. For at last our dimmed eyes are opened again. We see the Lord! The fact that he vanishes almost immediately from our sight and we no longer enjoy his physical presence does not trouble us. We have truly met him and we find no further cause for sorrow. We return at once, our spirits lightened and our hearts burning within us, to that city which has killed so many prophets, for we now know that there is one who has not succumbed to final death. We cannot wait to tell the others what happened on the way and how he was made known to us in the breaking of the bread. I too share in the joy of my two companions and I remember the eagerness of Mary also to tell this good news: "I have seen the Lord."

The meal shared at Emmaus is an experience which I have

recognized more than once, and sometimes in very surprising settings. I have a memory of a lunch with two friends, where I watched the one give to the other something she had needed but, being a single parent and barely making ends meet, had been unable to purchase. To stand and watch the giving and receiving of this gift was a transfixing experience. The surprise and gratitude of the one and the love and pleasure of the other at her friend's delight seemed to stop time for a moment. A simple event, to be sure, one which occurs often among good friends, I hope, but for me, the observer, the earth shook a bit—perhaps as it is described to have shaken for those who witnessed the Resurrection.

The meal we shared, after that moment had passed, had a transparent quality I shall never forget. We sat at a picnic table under maple trees in their full leaf of June. The sunlight, filtered through the leaves, made a dappled and flickering canopy of green above us. Our lunch was simple: crusty brown bread, the reddest of strawberries, a creamy yellow cheddar, and glasses of golden wine. I can still see the colors of the food and of the homegrown zinnias on the table. All had been made radiant and transfigured by the marvelous light. That the risen Lord was present with us, that he was there in the love of one friend's gift to another, that he too sat down at our table, and that it was on the very stuff of his life that we feasted that day—of all this none of us had any doubt. Whenever we have recalled that afternoon with one another or in the quiet of our own reflections, our hearts have burned within us and we know whom we met in the breaking of the bread. We can well exult: "We have seen the Lord!"

As Christians, we believe that Christ is truly risen, was seen by, and gave comfort to, his sorrowing friends and, in some mysterious way, is more truly present to us now than we can imagine. To describe this reality remains beyond our capacities, but our faith lets us proclaim with the author of the First Letter of John:

What was from the beginning,
what we have heard,
what we have seen with our eyes,
what we looked upon
and touched with our hands
concerns the Word of life—
for the life was made visible;
we have seen it and testify to it
and proclaim to you the eternal life
that was with the Father and was made visible to us—
what we have seen and heard
we proclaim now to you,
so that you too may have fellowship with us;
for our fellowship is with the Father
and with his Son, Jesus Christ.
We are writing this so that our joy may be complete.

(1 John 1:1-4)

Such truth we cannot enclose within our minds. We do not possess the Resurrection. But we are given the gift from time to time of seeing it and the commission of witnessing to it with our words and our lives.

Note

[1]"Gospel of Peter," par. 35-42, as quoted in Joseph A. Fitzmyer, S.J., *The Gospel According to Luke (X-XXIV)*, (New York: Doubleday, 1985), p. 1538.

Chapter Seven
"Take, Lord, Receive..."

The pages of the New Testament reveal an interesting paradox. Although we read there clear and exuberant testimony to the reality of the Resurrection, we do not receive a picture of the early Church living in unmitigated and triumphant joy. On the contrary, the letters of St. Paul and the Acts of the Aoostles expose factions, controversies, personal enmities, and sinfulness in the first Christian communities. They were as subject to confusion, ambition, rivalry, and discouragement as we are. Like us, they experienced a reality to which St. Paul alludes in the Letter to the Romans: that, although through baptism we have already now been united to Christ in his death, we hope for a future in which we will experience the glory of his resurrection:

> We were indeed buried with him through baptism into death, so that, just as Christ was raised from the dead by the glory of the Father, we too might live in newness of life.

> For if we have grown into union with him through a death like his, we shall also be united with him in the resurrection (Rom. 6:4-5).

The newness of life and the union with Christ in his resurrection consist in a promise, a hope, and an expectation. They color the Christian's vision, but they did not remove from the early Church, any more than they do from the Church today, the need to struggle with the demands and hardships of life and to confront its own sinfulness and failures. The life of the Church after the Resurrection is one of long-term engagement with earthiness where, in spite of its witness to the risen Lord, it will find within itself both sin and grace, sorrow and joy, confusion and clarity. For the Church of the New Testament, the tendency was to disregard the here and now of its situation in view of its expectation of the imminent return of Christ:

. . . the time is running out. From now on, let those having wives act as not having them, those weeping as not weeping, those rejoicing as not rejoicing, those buying as not owning, those using the world as not using it fully. For the world in its present form is passing away (1 Cor. 7:29-31).

The Church today is more likely to err in the opposite direction, expending itself in the exigencies of the present and occasionally losing sight of the promise and the hope. The reality of the Christian situation lies somewhere between these two extremes, in the knowledge that we already share in the life of Christ through baptism, but that we still groan as we wait for the full redemption of all creation (Rom. 8:18-25).

The person who has prayed the *Spiritual Exercises* through the contemplations of the fourth week on the Resurrection will be in a similar situation. Life goes on and the consolation of a real encounter with the risen Jesus will not remain a *felt* reality indefinitely. It may be obscured at times by the busyness, the demands, and the stresses of daily life. Sin and tragedy will continue to co-exist with the memory of, faith in, and hope for the Resurrection.

The movements of the soul throughout and beyond the *Spiritual Exercises* may be compared with a journey through various landscapes. It is not a coincidence that the Gospels record Jesus' preaching on a mountaintop, getting into a boat and crossing a lake, journeying to Jerusalem. St. Paul's travels over land and sea form the structural and thematic foundation of the Acts of the Apostles and parallel the development of that book's ecclesiology towards an understanding of the Christian mission to all the world.

In terms of an individual's life of faith, John Bunyan brilliantly traces Christian's wanderings over a series of helpful and dangerous landscapes in *The Pilgrim's Progress*. Ignatius is very insistent throughout the *Spiritual Exercises* that the retreatant practice the "composition of place," seeing in the imagination the place of the various events in the life of Jesus, and even the place of hell or heaven, as well as places in one's own life story.

One is then to put oneself into whatever place has been presented to the imagination.

When I think about my own experience of sin and grace in general, and of the Exercises in particular, I find that I too can associate God's action in my life with certain types of landscapes. Specifically I experience my journey as a Christian in terms of desert, mountains, the sea (water in general) and a garden.

Typically the desert is the place of desolation, but also of healing, self-knowledge, and growth. It parallels the experience of the first week of the Exercises where one is made to face one's sinfulness and bondage to all that is not God. In the desert one has an opportunity to put aside selfish attachments and to emerge with a renewed sense of one's need and desire for God alone. The deserts in my life are the times of loneliness, bereavement, failure, temptation, or confusion. They are not very comfortable but usually salutary.

It is good to remember that it is the Holy Spirit who led Jesus into the desert to be tempted by the devil. It was also by God's will that Moses led the people of Israel for forty years in the desert. During that time they learned their allegiance to the Lord alone. The desert is a barren and painful place, and Israel complains about the manna which is not so interesting over time as the cucumbers and garlic of Egypt:

> ...the Israelites lamented again, "Would that we had meat for food! We remember the fish we used to eat without cost in Egypt, and the cucumbers, the melons, the leeks, the onions, and the garlic. But now we are famished; we see nothing before us but this manna" (Num. 11:4-6).

The diet of the desert may indeed be tedious but it proves very nourishing and it does not upset the stomach. Over and over again we learn who we really are through our time spent in the desert—each time penetrating another false layer which has protected our true selves from our own awareness and the healing of God's grace. Such awareness and such healing bring not indigestion but peace of soul, a sure sign of the presence of God.

God, in fact, is not absent from the desert, although that may be our feeling about it. We cannot know our own sinfulness unless God reveals it to us in the environment of loving forgiveness. In the desert, Israel learns that it *wants* to be faithful to the covenant with the Lord. When tempted in the desert, Jesus clings to his Father and chooses the will of God rather than anything less. In Gethsemane (a garden which is really a desert) and on the cross (on a mountain which is really a desert), Jesus knows the utmost human weakness and desolation. He truly feels abandoned by God and yet, in precisely that abandonment, is fully united in obedience to his Father. In the desert we are out of control, and it is there that we are given the grace to let God be in control.

In my experience of the *Spiritual Exercises*, much of the contemplation during the second week takes place on a mountaintop. Jesus teaches the crowds there and calls for his followers to help in the work of building the Kingdom. He reigns from the cross on another mountain in the third week. I associate my mountain hike in Colorado with the "Principle and Foundation" which begins the Exercises, but that is actually an experience of water. It is the unexpected waterfall, in which I renew my baptism and which washes the scales from my eyes, which lets me see the Creator present in all the surrounding loveliness.

The mountain has always been a favored locus for theophany. Moses meets God directly on Mount Sinai and the people cannot bear to look upon the radiance of his face when he comes down among them (Ex. 34:29-35). In the Gospels, the disciples witness Jesus transfigured on Mount Tabor and are given insight into his divinity through the glory shining forth from his face and garments (Matt. 17:1-8; Mark 9:2-8; Luke 9:28-36). The ascension of Jesus to his Father is reported in Acts to take place from the Mount of Olives (Acts 1:6-12). To have been upon the mountain means in some way to have glimpsed transcendent glory, to have met God. The mountain is thus the place where we feel ourselves to be when we have experienced the grace of the fourth week: to know Jesus in the joy and victory of his resurrection.

But one may not remain upon the mountain forever. Eventually it becomes necessary to return to daily life. One lives in a world of ordinariness. It seems to me that this very fact may lie behind the design of Ignatius' final Exercise, the "Contemplation to Gain Love." He begins this Exercise with a statement on the nature of love:

> First, it is well to remark two things: the first is that love ought to be put more in deeds than in words.

> The second, love consists in interchange between the two parties; that is to say in the lover's giving and communicating to the beloved what he has or out of what he has or can; and so, on the contrary, the beloved to the lover. So that if the one has knowledge, he give to the one who has it not. The same of honors, of riches; and so the one to the other. [231]

We are to begin this Exercise by seeing ourselves in the presence of God and asking for the grace to know all that God has given, so that we may in gratitude return to God all that we have and are. There are four points for contemplation: God's particular gifts to us, the gift of God's dwelling in all creatures and in ourselves, God's working in all of creation, and the origin in God's goodness of all good that is in creation and in ourselves. In each case, the reflection on God's gifts to us is to evoke a desire to give all that is in us to God in return. As an expression of this response, Ignatius has written the very beautiful prayer:

> Take, Lord, and receive all my liberty, my memory, my understanding, and my entire will—all that I have and call my own. You have given it all to me. To you, Lord, I return it. Everything is yours; do with it what you will. Give me only your love and your grace. That is enough for me. [234][1]

The prayer of this contemplation on the love of God is, I believe, a response of the *Spiritual Exercises* for the "fifth week," i.e., the rest of one's life. The four points of the contemplation, touching as they do upon all of God's actions and goodness towards oneself and towards all of creation, have relevance to anything at all which can happen in a human life. There is nothing I can witness or experience which will not lead me back to one of those four points, if I but watch and listen carefully.

Such watching and listening most often takes place for me in the inner landscape of the garden. As is the case with Teresa's image of the watering of the garden, all sorts of activities take place there, from laborious hauling of water to the softness of rain. There is heavy spading to be done, weeding, fertilizing, transplanting, mulching—countless difficult chores. But sometimes there is little for the gardener to do. God provides the sun, the water, and the time in which things germinate, sprout, put forth leaves, blossoms, and eventually fruit. One receives the gift in a garden of watching the creation and the growth. One has the discipline of waiting patiently. Finally, one may forget oneself in a garden and become absorbed by the beauty and the life which matures there. In every bit of the garden, as in every moment of my life, the gift of God's very self is given for me. Every bit of experience—the joyous, the painful, the embarrassing, the tedious, and the foolish—all of it bears witness to the love of God. When I notice that this is so, then I will want to pray with Ignatius that the Lord take and receive my entire self.

That this is so is most clear to me in two very different experiences, one of the desert and one of the ocean. The first of these took place in a hospital—the desert in question. I had hepatitis and my worst symptom was an almost unbearable headache. Even the pillow hurt. In such a condition one cannot pray or even think very well. One just is. I knew that I wanted to pray, and probably that desire was the best thing I had to offer to the Lord at that moment. It was then that I experienced the gift of God's love to me in the midst of my own weakness, pain, and incapacity.

It seemed as if I stood before an open door full of light. The light, I knew, was Christ, though all I could see was just light. I felt him open his arms towards me and embrace me within this indescribable light. Then, having been taken thus into his very self, I next felt that he was pouring himself into me. This seemed like droplets of light or fire which filled me completely with a warmth that was almost physical. I had never before experienced being loved so profoundly or loving so deeply in return. The words of Ignatius' prayer spoke themselves within me. With all my being I said Yes to the gift of God's love in my life and knew that the substance of the moment in which I experienced that love had been one of pain. I loved the Lord in this *now* which was given to me, not because I was heroic at all, but simply because there was no other response to such overwhelming Love but Love Itself. The response was part of the gift and inseparable from it.

The second experience was vastly different from the first but, in an ultimate sense, not very different at all. I was snorkeling with my family over a coral reef in Hawaii. In no conventional sense was this a "religious" moment. What I experienced was a deep absorption in the unimaginable beauty of the water, the reef itself, and the fish. We floated effortlessly over myriads of brilliantly colored fish who neither fled us nor made any fuss at all over us, but simply swam by as if we were just some more unremarkable denizens of the sea. They would, however, eat bits of bread from our hands and would fight with each other over the food and even nibble at our fingers. I could have stayed forever, an awe-struck guest in a newly discovered world, watching the incredible grace, amazing diversity, and complete unselfconsciousness of these fish. There was neither past nor present, nor even much of myself that I was aware of then. I simply surrendered my whole self to gaze upon these lovely creatures into whose presence I had been privileged to enter.

Days later, moved by the beauty of tropical gardens, birds, flowers, and the amazingly blue ocean, I remembered how rapt I had been by the fish. I realized then that I now truly knew what I had only given intellectual assent to before: that it is of more value and has more to do with the purpose of my being here that I love the Christ who had touched me in my illness and the

God who had created so many species of fish, than that I do any other practical thing. In fact, to remain in this love is not at all separate from any "useful" tasks I may accomplish which are of immense "practical" value to the rest of the world.

Such an insight is very liberating. It is, of course, still necessary to make moral and vocational choices, to evaluate and make changes in one's lifestyle, to struggle for goodness and truthfulness and justice. All those things are very important. No one can honestly stand before God in prayer and not have within his or her range of vision all the evil and suffering in human life. Not to become engaged for good in the drama of history is an indication that one has not truly prayed. To remain with closed eyes and heart before the pain of God's people is not contemplation. The *Spiritual Exercises* of St. Ignatius presuppose a generous openness with our prayer and with our lives. God has placed us in the garden of creation that we may cultivate it, not let it go to seed. In fact, our work gives us great dignity. But the particular nature of our work within the garden, and how successful we are, is not of final importance. What is of final importance is that we remain in Love. The end of the *Spiritual Exercises* is to live in such freedom that nothing is withheld from Love, that we may say at each moment until our last:

> Take, Lord, and receive all my liberty, my memory, my understanding, and my entire will—all that I have and call my own. You have given it all to me. To you, Lord, I return it. Everything is yours; do with it what you will. Give me only your love and your grace. That is enough for me [234].[2]

Notes

[1] Fleming, p. 141.
[2] Fleming, p. 141.